I0818567

AN ILLUSTRATED GUIDE TO BIRDS THAT SOUND LIKE INSULTS.

LIBRARY OF CONGRESS CATALOGING-IN-PUBLICATION DATA AVAILABLE

ISBN 978-0-7353-8568-9

WRITTEN, DESIGNED, ILLUSTRATED, AND TYPESET BY MIKE SAYRE, MELANIE BRIDGES, JOHANNAH MILLER, ELLE BERGERHOFER, AND SPECIAL GUEST MARIAH MARKT. WE'RE EXHAUSTED.

10 9 8 7 6 5 4 3

SINCE YOU'RE STILL READING, HERE'S OUR RECIPE FOR MISSISSIPPI POT ROAST—YOU CAN THANK US LATER. PLACE A CHUCK ROAST IN A SLOW COOKER, THEN ADD A PACKET OF RANCH SEASONING, A PACKET OF AU JUS GRAVY MIX, A FEW PEPPERONCINI, AND A STICK OF BUTTER ON TOP. DON'T ADD WATER. COVER AND COOK ON LOW FOR 8 HOURS OR UNTIL THE MEAT IS TENDER AND EASILY SHREDDED. SERVE WITH MASHED POTATOES AND INVITE US OVER.

PRINTED IN CHINA.

BRASS MONKEY
1408 W. 12TH STREET
KANSAS CITY, MISSOURI 64101
WWW.BRASSMONKEYGOODS.COM

AN ILLUSTRATED GUIDE TO *Birds* THAT SOUND LIKE INSULTS.

BY BRASS MONKEY

A DISCLAIMER

× × ×

CONSIDER THIS BOOK TO BE FACTUAL-ISH.

THIS SHOULD PROBABLY COME AS NO SURPRISE IN A BOOK ABOUT RANDOM BIRDS THAT WE THINK SOUND LIKE INSULTS—BUT NOT EVERYTHING IN HERE IS ONE HUNDRED PERCENT ACCURATE.

WHILE WE TOOK CARE TO MAKE SURE THE BASIC FACTS OF EACH BIRD WERE ACCURATE, WE DO EMBELLISH THE TRUTH OCCASIONALLY IN THE NAME OF 'ENTERTAINMENT.' WE HOPE THAT THIS WILL BE OBVIOUS TO YOU, BUT IF YOU'RE UNSURE OF A 'FACT,' MAYBE LOOK IT UP ELSEWHERE BEFORE YOU CITE IT IN YOUR MASTER'S THESIS.

BY THE WAY, THE BIRDS ARE HAND-DRAWN TO BE FUNNY, NOT TO BE A REFERENCE IN ENCYCLOPEDIA BRITANNICA (IF THAT STILL EXISTS)—SO WE APOLOGIZE IN ADVANCE IF WE DIDN'T CAPTURE THE TRUE ESSENCE OF THE EYE-RINGS ON THE CHATTERING GNATWREN.

ANYWAY, WE HOPE YOU ENJOY IT.

BARE-CHEEKED BABBLER

TYPICALLY 9.5" LONG WITH A WHITE HEAD AND BELLY—AND FORGETTABLY BROWN WINGS AND STUFF. THE REAL STAR IS THEIR BIG CREEPY EYES THOUGH. IF A BIRD COULD SEE INTO THE AFTERLIFE, THIS ONE WOULD BE IT (SEE FIGURE 1).

SIGNATURE BIRD SONG

SOUNDS LIKE 'KERRRAKERRRA-KEK-KEK-KEK.' YOU KNOW, LIKE YOUR OLD CAR TRYING TO START.

PERFECT FOR INSULTING

- [ ] STREAKING STRANGERS
- [ ] NUDE SIGNIFICANT OTHERS
- [ ] NAKED MOLE RATS

FUN FACT: THEY ARE NAMED FOR THE VISIBLE BARE SKIN ON THEIR CHEEKS—WHICH THEY FEEL SUPER SELF-CONSCIOUS ABOUT, WE BET.

NATIVE AREAS

EXCLUSIVELY FOUND IN PARTS OF ANGOLA AND NAMIBIA—THAT'S RIGHT, THEY'VE SADLY NEVER SEEN AN ARBY'S.

PREFER TO USE THE LATIN BINOMIAL NAME? WELL IN THAT CASE, YOU SMELL LIKE A TURDOIDES GYMNOGENYS.

PUT ON SOME CLOTHES, YOU BARE-CHEEKED BABBLER.
FIG. 1

FIG. 2
NICE PARKING JOB, YOU ASH-BREASTED TIT-TYRANT.

ASH-BREASTED TIT-TYRANT

ROUGHLY 5" LONG AND MOSTLY GRAY, WITH A BLACK-ISH CROWN. WHEN NOT BUSY BEING A TIT-TYRANT, THEY'RE KNOWN TO SPEND THEIR TIME FLYING AROUND & SITTING ON BRANCHES. YOU KNOW—BIRD STUFF (SEE FIGURE 2).

SIGNATURE BIRD SONG

SOUNDS LIKE 'BREEEE DJR-DJR-DJR.' SO, KIND OF LIKE A MISSY ELLIOTT SONG—BUT PRETTY.

FUN FACT: WITH A POPULATION OF ONLY 200-900, THIS TIT-TYRANT IS ENDANGERED AND WOULD LIKELY DISPUTE THIS FACT BEING 'FUN.'

PERFECT FOR INSULTING

- FASHION DESIGNERS ☐
- CHIMNEY SWEEPS ☐
- HUGH HEFNER'S GHOST ☐

NATIVE AREAS

THEY ARE ONLY FOUND IN SELECT REGIONS OF PERU—EXCEPT FOR AN OCCASIONAL GIRLS' WEEKEND IN CABO.

PREFER TO USE THE LATIN BINOMIAL NAME? WOW, YOU SOUND LIKE A REAL ANAIRETES ALPINUS.

PAMPAS PIPIT

TYPICALLY 5" IN LENGTH WITH DISTINCT BROWN MARKINGS THAT ACT AS CAMOUFLAGE. THEY ARE PRIMARILY LAND BIRDS THAT SPEND THEIR TIME HOPPING AROUND, MINDING THEIR BUSINESS—SO MAYBE YOU SHOULD TOO (SEE FIGURE 3).

SIGNATURE BIRD SONG

MAKES A SOUND NOT UNLIKE AN OLD DIAL-UP MODEM STARTING UP. ASK YOUR PARENTS.

PERFECT FOR INSULTING

- [ ] SELF-PROCLAIMED FOODIES
- [ ] YOUR OLD BOSS
- [ ] YOUR NEW MOTHER-IN-LAW

FUN FACT: ONCE CLOSE TO BEING ENDANGERED IN THE LATE 80s, THEY'VE COME BACK STRONG—JUST LIKE ROBERT DOWNEY JR.

NATIVE AREAS

FOUND IN THE GRASSLANDS OF ARGENTINA, AN AREA KNOWN FOR ITS THRIVING AGRICULTURE—AND LIONEL MESSI.

PREFER TO USE THE LATIN BINOMIAL NAME? YEAH, YOU WOULD, YOU LITTLE ANTHUS CHACOENSIS.

UGH, STOP BEING SUCH A PAMPAS PIPIT.
FIG. 3

QUIT IT, YOU BLUE-FOOTED BOOBY.
FIG. 4

BLUE-FOOTED BOOBY

APPROXIMATELY 32" LONG WITH BRIGHT BLUE FEET, THESE WEIRDOS WOULD BE HARD TO MISS—IF THEY WEREN'T ALWAYS IN THE AIR. EXCEPT FOR WHEN THEY'RE TRYING TO MAKE MORE LITTLE BLUE-FOOTED BOOBIES, THAT IS (SEE FIGURE 4).

SIGNATURE BIRD SONG

NESTING MALES MAKE A 'PHEWWWW-PH-PHEWW-EW' SOUND—KINDA LIKE SOMEONE TRYING TO LEARN HOW TO WHISTLE.

FUN FACT: THEY ARE KNOWN TO ENJOY MULTIPLE PARTNERS EVERY MATING SEASON. MONOGAMY IS FOR LOSERS WITH BORING SHOES.

PERFECT FOR INSULTING

- UNATHLETIC FRIENDS ☐
- OLYMPIC BREAKDANCERS ☐
- SMURF COSPLAYERS ☐

NATIVE AREAS

THEY BREED IN THE TROPICAL AREAS ALONG THE EASTERN PACIFIC OCEAN—NOT UNLIKE COLLEGE SPRING BREAKERS.

PREFER TO USE THE LATIN BINOMIAL NAME? HAS ANYONE EVER TOLD YOU THAT YOU'RE A REAL SULA NEBOUXII?

COMMON CHIFFCHAFF

TYPICALLY 4" IN LENGTH AND BEST DESCRIBED LIKE A WOOD PENCIL: AVERAGE, BROWN, AND DULL. NO OFFENSE. THEY CAN FLY AND ALL OF THAT CRAP, AND WE'RE OVER HERE INSULTING BIRDS. POINT, COMMON CHIFFCHAFF (SEE FIGURE 5).

SIGNATURE BIRD SONG

MAKES A CONSTANT 'CHIFF-CHAFF CHIFF-CHAFF' SOUND—JUST LIKE A PAIR OF NEW SNEAKERS ON A GYM FLOOR.

PERFECT FOR INSULTING

- [ ] YOUR HOA PRESIDENT
- [ ] YOUR GOSSIPY COWORKERS
- [ ] ASSORTED STRAY DOGS

FUN FACT: THEY GET MISTAKEN FOR THE WILLOW WARBLER—WHICH IS GOOD TO KNOW IN CASE YOU WANT TO FRAME A BIRD FOR MURDER.

NATIVE AREAS

FOUND IN WOODED HABITATS ACROSS EUROPE DURING THE SUMMER, BUT SPEND THEIR WINTERS IN ASIA—MUST BE NICE.

OH, YOU PREFER TO USE THE LATIN BINOMIAL NAME? STOP BEING SUCH A PHYLLOSCOPUS COLLYBITA.

FIG. 5
CALM DOWN, YOU COMMON CHIFFCHAFF.

FIG. 6
PAY ME BACK, YOU YELLOW-BELLIED SAPSUCKER.

YELLOW-BELLIED SAPSUCKER

AROUND 7" IN LENGTH WITH A RED HEAD, BLACK AND WHITE WINGS, AND—YOU GUESSED IT—A YELLOW BELLY. OH, IT ALSO SUCKS SAP. SERIOUSLY, HOW DO YOU GET ON THE BIRD NAMING COMMITTEE? THAT SOUNDS EASY (SEE FIGURE 6).

SIGNATURE BIRD CALL

MAKES A 'QUEE-AH QUEE-AH' NOISE. SORT OF LIKE A SQUEAKY DOG TOY—WHICH THEY ALSO TRY HARD TO AVOID BECOMING.

FUN FACT: THEY BEAT ON DEAD TREES IN ORDER TO COMMUNICATE WITH FELLOW SAPSUCKERS—SO AN AVERAGE DRUM CIRCLE, REALLY.

PERFECT FOR INSULTING

- [ ] BROKEN DOWN CARS
- [ ] SIGNIFICANTLY OLDER EXES
- [ ] PIKACHU

NATIVE AREAS

FOUND MOSTLY IN CANADA—HOME OF THE MIGHTY MAPLE TREE. SAPSUCKERS ARE REAL 'BREAKFAST FOR DINNER' TYPES.

OH, YOU PREFER THE LATIN BINOMIAL NAME? WHY AM I NOT SURPRISED, YOU SPHYRAPICUS VARIUS.

BUSHTIT

TYPICALLY 4" LONG—AND, HONESTLY, MOST OF THAT IS TAIL. OTHERWISE, THEIR BIG HEAD MERGES INTO A PUFFY, ROUND BODY THAT RESEMBLES A BALD MIDDLE MANAGER WITH A DOUBLE CHIN—PROBABLY NAMED 'LARRY' (SEE FIGURE 7).

SIGNATURE BIRD SONG

MAKES A SHORT, HIGH-PITCHED 'PSST-PSST-PSST' SOUND—LIKE AN OLD-TIMEY GANGSTER TRYING TO TELL YOU A SECRET.

PERFECT FOR INSULTING

- ☐ MALL WALKERS
- ☐ BAD TOPIARY GARDENERS
- ☐ ELDERLY DRIVERS

FUN FACT: MALE BUSHTITS ARE VERY ACTIVE PARENTS. THEY HELP BUILD NESTS, FIND FOOD, AND TEACH THE YOUNG—AND GET #1 BUSHTIT MUGS.

NATIVE AREAS

FOUND IN THE WESTERN UNITED STATES, MEXICO, AND EVEN SOMETIMES CANADA—PRESUMABLY IF THEY ARE INTO HOCKEY.

PSALTRIPARUS MINIMUS—THAT'S EITHER THE LATIN BINOMIAL NAME OR A BUDGET WIZARD SPELL.

MOVE IT,
BUSHTIT.
FIG. 7

YOUR MOM IS A HAIRY-BREASTED BARBET.
FIG. 8

HAIRY-BREASTED BARBET

TYPICALLY 6 TO 7" LONG—BUT A SOLID 8" ON DATING APPS. WHILE THEIR WINGS ARE BLACK WITH YELLOW SPOTTING, THEIR BELLY IS YELLOW WITH BLACK SPOTTING—KIND OF LIKE HOW YOUR ART TEACHER IN FIRST GRADE DRESSED (SEE FIGURE 8).

SIGNATURE BIRD SONG

SOUNDS LIKE SOMEONE SAYING 'OOH-OOH-OOH' SLOWLY INTO A MICROPHONE—LIKE A REALLY LOW-ENERGY HYPE MAN.

FUN FACT: THEY LIKE TO REMOVE THE WINGS AND LEGS OF INSECTS BEFORE THEY EAT THEM—BY BASHING THEM AGAINST TREES. FUN.

PERFECT FOR INSULTING

- NEWBORN BABIES ☐
- MIDDLE SCHOOL BULLIES ☐
- TOM SELLECK ☐

NATIVE AREAS

CAN BE FOUND IN WESTERN AND CENTRAL AFRICA—WHERE MANY CLAIM TO HAVE BEEN EXTRAS IN 'THE LION KING.'

TRICHOLAEMA HIRSUTA—THAT'S EITHER THE LATIN BINOMIAL NAME OR WHAT YOU CAME DOWN WITH LAST WINTER.

MARBLED GODWIT

IF YOU THINK YOU SEE A DUCK WEARING STILTS, DON'T BE DISAPPOINTED, BUT IT'S PROBABLY JUST ONE OF THESE THINGS. MEASURING 16 TO 20" LONG, THEIR STICK-FIGURE LEGS PAIR PERFECTLY WITH THEIR WEIRD BEAKS (SEE FIGURE 9).

SIGNATURE BIRD SONG

SOUNDS LIKE A GUTTURAL 'GERRR-RHIT'—KIND OF LIKE A RECORD SCRATCH FROM A TERRIBLE WEDDING DJ.

PERFECT FOR INSULTING

- ☐ GROUP PROJECT PARTNERS
- ☐ CLUELESS INTERNS
- ☐ YOUR DAD USING AN iPHONE

FUN FACT: THE MARBLED GODWIT BREEDS WITH THE SAME PARTNER EVERY YEAR—AND THEN GETS TO BE BLISSFULLY ALONE FOR 12 MONTHS.

NATIVE AREAS

THEY MAINLY RESIDE ALONG THE SHORES OF NORTH AMERICA—AND LIKELY HAVE 'SALT LIFE' STICKERS ON THEIR CARS.

LIMOSA FEDOA—THAT'S EITHER THE LATIN BINOMIAL NAME OR THE TYPE OF HAT MARGARITA DRINKERS WEAR.

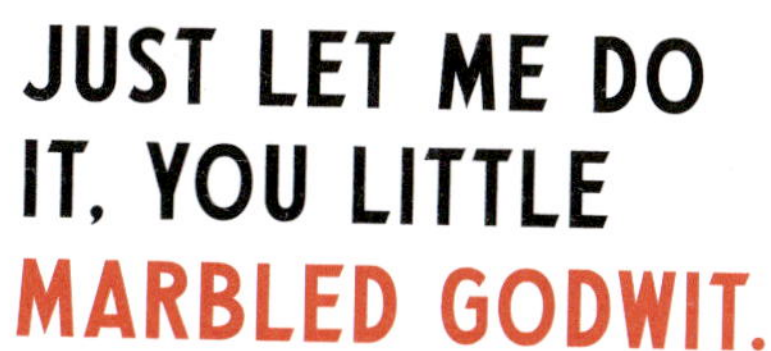

FIG. 9

SMOOTH MOVE, YOU THREE-TOED JACAMAR.
FIG. 10

THREE-TOED JACAMAR

TYPICALLY AROUND 7" IN LENGTH—BUT LET'S BE HONEST, MOST OF THAT IS BEAK. THEY'RE ALSO THE ONLY BREED OF JACAMAR WITH THREE TOES, SO THEY PROBABLY HAVE A REALLY HARD TIME FINDING SHOES (SEE FIGURE 10).

SIGNATURE BIRD SONG

YOU KNOW WHEN YOU'RE DRIVING CROSS-COUNTRY AND THE RADIO STATION GOES OUT OF TUNE? THAT.

FUN FACT: THE MALE BIRDS SING IN GROUPS OF 3 TO 6. SO THEY'RE JUST A SLEAZY MANAGER AWAY FROM A COCAINE PROBLEM.

PERFECT FOR INSULTING

- COMPETITIVE DANCERS ☐
- CLUMSY RUNWAY MODELS ☐
- TOE-SHOE WEARERS ☐

NATIVE AREAS

THEY ARE EXCLUSIVELY FOUND IN THE SOUTHEASTERN REGION OF BRAZIL—THAT IS UNLESS ONE GOT REALLY, REALLY LOST.

PREFER TO USE THE LATIN BINOMIAL NAME? I ALWAYS KNEW YOU WERE A JACAMARALCYON TRIDACTYLA.

WOODCOCK

USUALLY 10 TO 12" IN LENGTH, WOODCOCKS ARE MOST KNOWN FOR THEIR WALK. THINK 70s-ERA JOHN TRAVOLTA, EXCEPT THEY EAT EARTHWORMS. WHICH, TO OUR KNOWLEDGE, WERE NOT ON THE 'GREASE' CATERING TABLE (SEE FIGURE 11).

SIGNATURE BIRD SONG

MAKES KIND OF A SHORT 'EEEEEH' SOUND, LIKE THE BUZZER FOR A WRONG ANSWER ON A GAME SHOW, BUT CUTE.

PERFECT FOR INSULTING

- [ ] PINOCCHIO
- [ ] VARIOUS SCARECROWS
- [ ] ELIJAH WOOD

FUN FACT: IF THEY SENSE DANGER, THEY FREEZE AND PRAY THAT NO ONE CAN SEE THEM—KINDA LIKE WHEN YOU SEE YOUR BOSS AT TARGET.

NATIVE AREAS

FOUND IN WOODED AREAS IN THE SOUTHEASTERN UNITED STATES. SO, BASICALLY ANYWHERE THERE'S A PIGGLY WIGGLY.

OH, YOU PREFER THE LATIN BINOMIAL NAME? I BET YOU WERE A REAL SCOLOPAX MINOR IN HIGH SCHOOL.

THAT WASN'T SUBTLE, YOU WOODCOCK.
FIG. 11

FIG. 12

CRYPTIC WARBLER

AT AROUND 4" LONG, WITH A SMALL, ROUND BODY, IT'S RUMORED THAT PEEPS WERE MODELED AFTER THEM. THE TASTE OF PEEPS, HOWEVER, WAS INSPIRED BY A CLUMP OF WET SAND, DROPPED IN SPLENDA (SEE FIGURE 12).

SIGNATURE BIRD SONG

SOUNDS LIKE A QUICK, CONSECUTIVE 'DEET-DEET-DEET-DEET,' LIKE THE CAR ALARM ON THAT 2013 BUICK YOU PARKED BY.

FUN FACT: THEY WERE IDENTIFIED AS A SPECIES IN 1992, WHICH KIND OF MAKES THEM MILLENNIALS. THAT, AND THEIR LOVE OF AVOCADO TOAST.

PERFECT FOR INSULTING

- LONG-WINDED TEXTERS ☐
- THE WRITERS OF 'LOST' ☐
- YOUR OLD MATH TEACHER ☐

NATIVE AREAS

THEY'RE MOSTLY FOUND IN EASTERN MADAGASCAR—UNLESS DELTA IS RUNNING A SALE OR SOMETHING.

LOOKING FOR THE LATIN BINOMIAL NAME? GOOD LUCK, YOU CRYPTOSYLVICOLA RANDRIANASOLOI.

CRESTED JAYSHRIKE

TYPICALLY 12" LONG—WITH MOST OF THAT COMING FROM THAT FANCY CREST ON THEIR HEAD. WHILE THEIR BODIES ARE MOSTLY DARK, THEY'VE GOT A BRIGHT WHITE COLLAR—YOU KNOW, LIKE A BIRD PRIEST OR SOMETHING (SEE FIGURE 13).

SIGNATURE BIRD SONG

MAKES A 'TEEEE-WOOOOOO' SOUND THAT STARTS OUT HIGH AND ENDS LOW—KINDA LIKE A VACUUM BEING TURNED OFF.

PERFECT FOR INSULTING

- ☐ SERIAL INTERRUPTERS
- ☐ SELF-PROCLAIMED ALPHAS
- ☐ CHRONIC WHISTLERS

FUN FACT: THEIR CALL CLOSELY RESEMBLES THE SOUND OF A MACHINE GUN—IN CASE RAMBO IS LOOKING FOR WHITE NOISE.

NATIVE AREAS

MOSTLY FOUND IN THE TROPICAL FORESTS OF THAILAND, MALAYSIA, AND MYANMAR—PROBABLY JUDGING THE TOURISTS.

OH, YOU PREFER TO USE THE LATIN BINOMIAL NAME? YOU'RE SO FULL OF PLATYLOPHUS GALERICULATUS.

NO ONE CARES, YOU CRESTED JAYSHRIKE.
FIG. 13

FIG. 14

SCALE-THROATED EARTHCREEPER

ROUGHLY 8" LONG—WHICH IS TOTALLY ABOVE AVERAGE, BY THE WAY. OTHERWISE THEY'RE MOSTLY BROWN, WITH SOME BUSHY BIRD-EYEBROWS THAT ARE ALARMINGLY SIMILAR TO MARTIN SCORSESE'S (SEE FIGURE 14).

SIGNATURE BIRD SONG

THEY MAKE A SQUEALING 'EE-EE-E-EE' SOUND, LIKE SOMEONE USING AN ALMOST-EMPTY DRY ERASE MARKER IN A TREE.

FUN FACT: THEY LAY THEIR EGGS IN TUNNELS INSTEAD OF JUST BUILDING NESTS IN TREES LIKE NORMAL BIRDS. UGH, WE GET IT. YOU'RE UNIQUE.

PERFECT FOR INSULTING

- SLOT MACHINE PLAYERS ☐
- DENTAL HYGIENISTS ☐
- PUFF, THE MAGIC DRAGON ☐

NATIVE AREAS

WHILE MOSTLY YEAR-ROUND RESIDENTS OF SOUTHERN CHILE AND ARGENTINA, RUMOR HAS IT THAT A FEW OF THEM FELL FOR TIME-SHARES IN URUGUAY. THOSE CONTRACTS ARE A REAL NIGHTMARE TO GET OUT OF.

FAN-TAILED BERRYPECKER

WHILE GENERALLY 5 TO 6" LONG, THE FEMALES ARE OFTEN LARGER THAN THE MALES. NEED A VISUAL AID? JUST PICTURE JOE JONAS WITH EVERY GIRL THAT HE'S EVER DATED (SEE FIGURE 15).

SIGNATURE BIRD SONG

SOUNDS LIKE A REPETITIVE, NASALLY 'WEH' SOUND. KIND OF LIKE A BABY. OR BOB DYLAN. OR BOTH.

PERFECT FOR INSULTING

- ☐ STRICT VEGETARIANS
- ☐ FARMER'S MARKET SHOPPERS
- ☐ HALLE BERRY'S BOYFRIEND

FUN FACT: THEY PRIMARILY EAT BERRIES—WHICH EXPLAINS THEIR NAME. UNLIKE THE FAN-TAILED PEPPERONI-HOT POCKET-PECKER.

NATIVE AREAS

PRIMARILY FOUND IN THE TROPICAL MONTANE FORESTS OF NEW GUINEA. ADORABLY PRETENTIOUS, JUST LIKE THE BIRDS.

MELANOCHARIS VERSTERI—THAT'S EITHER THE LATIN BINOMIAL NAME OR A REALLY BORING FASHION DESIGNER.

GET OVER IT, YOU FAN-TAILED BERRYPECKER.
FIG. 15

FIG. 16
LAH-TEE-DAH. YOU CAN BE SUCH A TUFTED TITMOUSE.

TUFTED TITMOUSE

ROUGHLY 5 TO 6" LONG, THEY'RE MOSTLY GRAY ON TOP AND WHITE BELOW, WITH ORANGISH BLOTCHES ON THEIR SIDES THAT ARE STRIKINGLY SIMILAR TO THE CHEETOS STAINS ON OUR FINGERS (SEE FIGURE 16).

SIGNATURE BIRD SONG

IMAGINE THAT YOUR NAME IS PETER. NOW IMAGINE THAT A SIX-YEAR-OLD WANTS YOUR ATTENTION. 'PETER-PETER-PETER.'

FUN FACT: THEY ARE KNOWN FOR KLEPTOTRICHY–THAT'S PULLING THE HAIR OUT OF LIVE MAMMALS LIKE CATS. AND JUDE LAW.

PERFECT FOR INSULTING

- PUSH-UP BRA WEARERS ☐
- BRATTY TEENAGERS ☐
- ANYONE ON LINKEDIN ☐

NATIVE AREAS

NATIVE TO EASTERN NORTH AMERICA, THEY CAN BE SPOTTED SPORTING PASTEL SHORTS AND SAILING OFF NANTUCKET.

BAEOLOPHUS BICOLOR–THAT'S EITHER THE LATIN BINOMIAL NAME OR SOME WEIRD SPECIES OF POKÉMON.

BARNACLE GOOSE

RANGING FROM 22 TO 28" LONG, THESE MONSTERS SPORT A WHITE HEAD AND BELLY—WHICH PERFECTLY ACCENTUATE THEIR BLACK EYE MARKINGS. THINK THE GOTH KIDS WORKING AT HOT TOPIC, BUT WITH MORE FEATHERS (SEE FIGURE 17).

SIGNATURE BIRD SONG

THAT SQUEAKY SOUND WET RUBBER BOOTS MAKE WHEN YOU'RE JUST TRYING TO WALK THROUGH THE GROCERY STORE.

PERFECT FOR INSULTING

- [ ] AN OVERLY CLINGY FRIEND
- [ ] A CHILD LEARNING ANYTHING
- [ ] TOM CRUISE'S CO-WORKERS

FUN FACT: NEW HATCHLINGS JUMP OFF OF CLIFFS FOR FOOD JUST DAYS AFTER THEY HATCH. MEANWHILE, WE STILL EAT UNCRUSTABLES.

NATIVE AREAS

THEY MAINLY LIVE IN EUROPE, BUT MIGRATE TO GREENLAND, SVALBARD, AND RUSSIA TO BREED—AND GET GOOD VODKA.

PREFER TO USE THE LATIN BINOMIAL NAME? IT SOUNDS LIKE YOU'VE GOT A BAD CASE OF BRANTA LEUCOPSIS.

YOUR BRAIN IS A MARVEL, YOU BARNACLE GOOSE.

FIG. 17

TRY AGAIN, YOU MARBLED FROGMOUTH.
FIG. 18

MARBLED FROGMOUTH

ROUGHLY 12 TO 18" TALL, AND MOSTLY BROWN WITH MOTTLED MARKINGS. THEIR MOST PROMINENT FEATURE IS THEIR WIDE, FROG-LIKE BILL, BUT UNLIKE IN FAIRY TALES, KISSING THEM WILL HAVE MIXED RESULTS AT BEST (SEE FIGURE 18).

SIGNATURE BIRD SONG

SOUNDS LIKE A TURKEY GOBBLING AND GETTING ITS HEAD CHOPPED OFF. WHAT FUN THANKSGIVING TABLE TRIVIA.

FUN FACT: DURING THE DAYTIME, THEY CAMOUFLAGE THEMSELVES AS BROKEN BRANCHES—WHICH CAN'T DO MUCH FOR THEIR SELF-ESTEEM.

PERFECT FOR INSULTING

- MOVIE THEATER TALKERS ☐
- DRUNK UNCLES ☐
- BLACK MARKET KERMITS ☐

NATIVE AREAS

PRIMARILY FOUND IN PAPUA NEW GUINEA, BUT OCCASIONALLY MAKE IT TO AUSTRALIA—FOR VEGEMITE, WE'RE GUESSING.

PODARGUS OCELLATUS—THAT'S EITHER THE LATIN BINOMIAL NAME OR SOME KIND OF TOENAIL FUNGUS.

YELLOW-BILLED CUCKOO

MEASURING 10 TO 12" LONG, WITH A BROWN BACK AND WHITE BELLY, THEY'RE DISTINCTIVE FOR THEIR TERRIBLE POSTURE—OFTEN SITTING HUNCHED OVER IN TREES TO CONCEAL THEIR STOMACHS. NOT UNLIKE US (SEE FIGURE 19).

SIGNATURE BIRD SONG

THAT RATTLE THAT A CAN OF SPRAY PAINT MAKES WHILE YOU STRUGGLE TO SHAKE IT FOR 60 SECONDS BEFORE USE.

PERFECT FOR INSULTING

- ☐ NYC TAXI DRIVERS
- ☐ PEOPLE WITH BIG NOSES
- ☐ YOUR CHEATING EX

FUN FACT: IT ONLY TAKES 17 DAYS FOR A NEWLY LAID EGG TO HATCH AND LEAVE THE NEST—AND PROBABLY CAUSE ITS PARENTS TO GROW APART.

NATIVE AREAS

USUALLY FOUND IN THE EASTERN AND CENTRAL REGIONS OF THE U.S.—JUST LIKE CRACKER BARREL. COINCIDENCE?

COCCYZUS AMERICANUS—THAT'S EITHER THE LATIN BINOMIAL NAME OR AN STD ONLY AMERICANS CAN CONTRACT.

THE EARTH IS ROUND, YOU YELLOW-BILLED CUCKOO.
FIG. 19

WHAT'S THAT SUPPOSED TO MEAN, YOU ASHY TIT?
FIG. 20

ASHY TIT

USUALLY 6" IN LENGTH, WITH A GRAY BODY AND BLACK HEAD. BUT THANKS TO THE WHITE STREAKS ON THEIR FACE, THEY LOOK LIKE THEY JUST CHUGGED MILK STRAIGHT FROM THE CARTON. NOT THAT WE'D KNOW (SEE FIGURE 20).

SIGNATURE BIRD SONG

ESSENTIALLY THE SOUND THAT WALMART'S ANTITHEFT SENSORS MAKE WHEN THEY FORGET TO TAKE THE TAGS OFF.

FUN FACT: THEY'RE RESIDENT BIRDS, WHICH MEANS THAT THEY DON'T MIGRATE. WHICH IS KIND OF LIKE US AFTER 7PM ON WEEKNIGHTS.

PERFECT FOR INSULTING

- THE VICTIMS OF POMPEII ☐
- CHAIN-SMOKERS ☐
- BERT FROM 'MARY POPPINS' ☐

NATIVE AREAS

FOUND IN ANGOLA, BOTSWANA, NAMIBIA, AND ZIMBABWE, LIKELY DOING THEIR BEST TO AVOID THAT TOTO SONG.

PREFER TO USE THE LATIN BINOMIAL NAME? YOU'RE PREACHING TO THE CHOIR, YOU MELANIPARUS CINERASCENS.

FLAMMULATED OWL

MEASURING AROUND 6" IN LENGTH, THESE ALREADY CREEPY-LOOKING BIRDS ARE MADE EXTRA-CREEPY THANKS TO THEIR GIANT EYEBALLS CRAMMED INTO AN EXCEPTIONALLY TINY, JUICE-CAN-SIZED BODY (SEE FIGURE 21).

SIGNATURE BIRD SONG

A LOW, MONOTONOUS HONK—SORT OF LIKE A PHONE BUZZING ON A PLASTIC LAWN CHAIR. REPEATEDLY. FOR HOURS.

PERFECT FOR INSULTING

- ☐ WOMEN IN MENOPAUSE
- ☐ TOOTSIE POP FANS
- ☐ HOOTERS EMPLOYEES

FUN FACT: THEY ARE EXTREMELY LOUD FOR THEIR SIZE—WHICH KINDA SOUNDS LIKE THEY'RE COMPENSATING FOR SOMETHING.

NATIVE AREAS

FOUND IN THE U.S. AND CANADA, THESE BIRDS MIGRATE TO CENTRAL AMERICA FOR THE WINTER—LIKE YOUR SINGLE AUNT.

OH, YOU PREFER TO USE THE LATIN BINOMIAL NAME? SPOKEN LIKE A TRUE PSILOSCOPS FLAMMEOLUS.

WAY TO GO, YOU
FLAMMULATED OWL.

FIG. 21

TAKE A HIKE, YOU WESTERN WOOD PEWEE.
FIG. 22

WESTERN WOOD PEWEE

ROUGHLY 5 TO 6" LONG, THESE DRAB GRAYISH-GREEN BIRDS ARE EXCEPTIONAL IN THEIR PLAINNESS. JUST LIKE AN OLD HIGH SCHOOL BOYFRIEND, THEY'RE FAMILIAR, SAFE, AND OH-SO-WONDERFULLY FORGETTABLE (SEE FIGURE 22).

SIGNATURE BIRD SONG

A LOUD BUZZY 'BREEERR' THAT SOUNDS SO MUCH LIKE A GYM TEACHER WHISTLE, IT SHOULD COME WITH A TRIGGER WARNING.

FUN FACT: THEY ARE SIT-AND-WAIT PREDATORS WHEN IT COMES TO FINDING FOOD—AND OUR DOORDASH ACCOUNT NODS IN SOLIDARITY.

PERFECT FOR INSULTING

- MIDDLE SCHOOLERS ☐
- NATURAL DEODORANT USERS ☐
- ANYONE AFTER CARDIO ☐

NATIVE AREAS

KNOWN FOR LIVING (AND BREEDING) IN THE WOODS OF THE WESTERN UNITED STATES—JUST LIKE ANY TRUE HIPSTER.

CONTOPUS SORDIDULUS—THAT'S EITHER THE LATIN BINOMIAL NAME OR A HIGHLY RANKED MILITARY OCTOPUS.

AMAZONIAN GROSBEAK

MEASURING ROUGHLY 6" LONG, THE MALES OF THE SPECIES ARE VIBRANT SHADES OF BLUE—WHILE THE FEMALES ARE ALL BROWN. THEY ALSO PAY MORE ON CAR INSURANCE DESPITE BEING SAFER DRIVERS (SEE FIGURE 23).

SIGNATURE BIRD SONG

AN OFF-KEY 'PEE-TEE-TU-TU-TI-PEE-CHEE' SOUND, BEST DESCRIBED AS A SIM TRYING TO SING A TAYLOR SWIFT SONG.

PERFECT FOR INSULTING

- [ ] KIDS WITH RUNNY NOSES
- [ ] PEOPLE OVER 6 FEET TALL
- [ ] JEFF BEZOS

FUN FACT: THEY ARE MEMBERS OF THE CARDINAL FAMILY—JUST ONES THAT NOBODY LIKES TO TALK ABOUT.

NATIVE AREAS

THEY'RE WIDELY DISTRIBUTED IN THE AMAZON BASIN—BUT THAT'S PROBABLY THANKS TO A DISCOUNT ON PRIME.

PREFER TO USE THE LATIN BINOMIAL NAME? WOW, YOUR MOTHER RAISED A REAL CYANOLOXIA ROTHSCHILDII.

FIG. 23
I'M DOWN HERE, YOU AMAZONIAN GROSBEAK.

FIG. 24

BEARDED SCRUB ROBIN

ROUGHLY 6 TO 7" LONG, WITH BOLD WHITE STRIPES ON THEIR FACE. COINCIDENTLY, THIS IS ALSO WHAT WE CALL DOCTORS THAT REFUSE TO CHANGE OUT OF THEIR HOSPITAL GARB BEFORE GOING TO THE BAR AFTER WORK (SEE FIGURE 24).

SIGNATURE BIRD SONG

THEIR CALLS INCLUDE 'CHRRRT,' 'CHEK-CHEK-KWEZZZZZZZ,' AND 'SEEEEP'—JUST LIKE YOUR BEATBOXING COUSIN.

FUN FACT: THEY ARE BOTH MONOGAMOUS AND TERRITORIAL. UGH, EVERY WOMAN'S DREAM.

PERFECT FOR INSULTING

- A GUY THAT THINKS HE'S FLY ☐
- A GUY THAT'S ALSO A BUSTA ☐
- WHOEVER ELSE TLC SAID ☐

NATIVE AREAS

EXCLUSIVELY FOUND IN THE SOUTHEASTERN REGIONS OF AFRICA—BUT THEY'RE ALWAYS CHECKING ZILLOW LISTINGS.

TYCHAEDON QUADRIVIRGATA—THAT'S EITHER THE LATIN BINOMIAL NAME OR A FORGOTTEN SHAPE FROM GEOMETRY.

LESSER YELLOWLEGS

TYPICALLY 9.5" LONG, WITH GRAYISH BROWN STREAKING. HOWEVER, THEY'RE REALLY MOST NOTABLE FOR THEIR VIVID ORANGISH-YELLOW LEGS. IF IT WAS A COLOR AT BENJAMIN MOORE, WE'D CALL IT 'OOMPA-LOOMPA.' (SEE FIGURE 25).

SIGNATURE BIRD SONG

A HIGH-PITCHED, REPETITIVE 'TEW-TEW-TEW' SOUND—LIKE THOSE LASER GUNS IN B-MOVIES FROM THE 80s.

PERFECT FOR INSULTING

- ☐ CHRONIC SPRAY-TANNERS
- ☐ INDOOR FRIENDS ON A HIKE
- ☐ SPONGEBOB

FUN FACT: THEY MIGRATE NONSTOP, TRAVELING UP TO 4,350 MILES WITHOUT A BREAK. SO, JUST LIKE A SUMMER ROAD TRIP WITH DAD.

NATIVE AREAS

MOST SPEND WINTER IN SOUTH AMERICA BEFORE TRAVELING TO CANADA TO BREED. IT'S COLD, WHAT ELSE IS THERE TO DO?

TRINGA FLAVIPES—THAT'S EITHER THE LATIN BINOMIAL NAME OR AN ECCENTRIC BAGPIPE PLAYER.

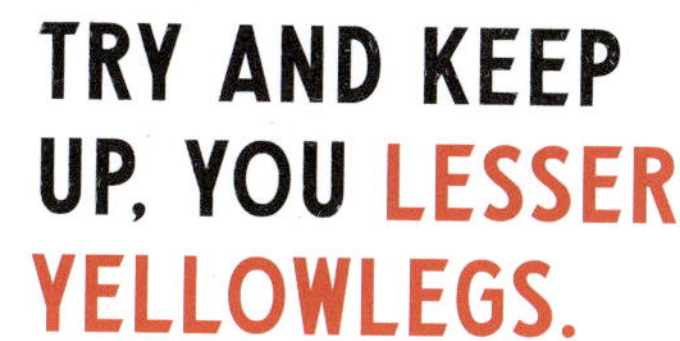

FIG. 25

FIG. 26

PARASITIC JAEGER

MEASURING 16 TO 19" IN LENGTH, THESE BIRDS HAVE TWO DISTINCT COLOR MORPHS. SOME ARE A DARK GRAY TONE, WHILE OTHERS ARE A LIGHTER BEIGE COLOR. BUT AS THEY SAY, 'BEIGE MORPHS HAVE MORE FUN' (SEE FIGURE 26).

SIGNATURE BIRD SONG

A SERIES OF NASAL 'YEEW-YEEW-YEEW' NOISES THAT MOSTLY JUST SOUND LIKE SNOOPY LAUGHING AT SOMETHING.

FUN FACT: THEY ARE OFFICIALLY KLEPTOPARASITES– WHICH MEANS THAT THEY STEAL FOOD TO SURVIVE. LIKE YOUR OLD ROOMMATE.

PERFECT FOR INSULTING

- YOUR FRIEND'S EX-HUSBAND ☐
- PATRICK MAHOMES' BROTHER ☐
- SPAM CALLERS ☐

NATIVE AREAS

THEY OFTEN MIGRATE BETWEEN THE ARCTIC TUNDRA AND THE SOUTHERN TROPICS–SO PACKING MUST BE A NIGHTMARE.

PREFER TO USE THE LATIN BINOMIAL NAME? JUST STAY AWAY FROM ME, YOU STERCORARIUS PARASITICUS.

DICKCISSEL

TYPICALLY 5 TO 6" LONG, BUT ON THE HIGHER SIDE IF YOU TAKE THEIR WORD FOR IT. THEY'RE MOSTLY GRAY AND BROWN, WITH RUST PATCHES ON THEIR WINGS—AND KNOWN TO SEND OUT UNSOLICITED PHOTOS (SEE FIGURE 27).

SIGNATURE BIRD SONG

A 'DICK-DICK-CISS-CISS-CISS' SOUND—ODDLY SIMILAR TO THE LYRICS OF AN AVERAGE CUPCAKKE SONG.

PERFECT FOR INSULTING

- [ ] MANSPLAINERS
- [ ] CARS THAT CUT YOU OFF
- [ ] SISSY SPACEK

FUN FACT: MALES MATE WITH UP TO 6 FEMALES PER SEASON—SO THERE IS A NON-ZERO CHANCE THAT THEY ARE RELATED TO NICK CANNON.

NATIVE AREAS

FOUND IN THE GRASSLANDS OF THE U.S. MIDWEST. LOOK, WE LIVE HERE—IT'S CRAWLING WITH DICKCISSELS. BIRDS, TOO.

OH, YOU PREFER TO USE THE LATIN BINOMIAL NAME? WELL THAT DOESN'T SOUND VERY SPIZA AMERICANA OF YOU.

FIG. 27
SURE THING,
YOU LITTLE
DICKCISSEL.

FIG. 28

LONG-LEGGED BUZZARD

THEY'RE 5" LONG AND MOSTLY GRAY. BUT MORE IMPORTANTLY, THEY HAVE DISAPPOINTINGLY SHORT LEGS FOR SOMETHING THAT BILLS ITSELF AS A LONG-LEGGED BUZZARD. GET BACK TO US WHEN THEY LOOK LIKE CHOPSTICKS (SEE FIGURE 28).

SIGNATURE BIRD SONG

YOU KNOW THE SOUND YOUR CAT MAKES WHEN IT WANTS TO BE FED? PRETTY MUCH THAT, BUT SLIGHTLY MORE TERRIFYING.

FUN FACT: THE FEMALES CAN BE 30 PERCENT HEAVIER THAN THE MALES—BUT IT'S PROBABLY A GOOD IDEA NOT TO MENTION IT.

PERFECT FOR INSULTING

- CLOWNS ON STILTS ☐
- RUDE BASKETBALL PLAYERS ☐
- JACK SKELLINGTON ☐

NATIVE AREAS

FOUND WIDELY ACROSS EURASIA AND NORTH AFRICA, THEY'RE ESSENTIALLY A BUDGET BALD EAGLE.

BUTEO RUFINUS—THAT'S EITHER THE LATIN BINOMIAL NAME OR SOME RICH FAMILY'S PET DOG.

MOUSTACHED WOODCREEPER

MEASURING 11 TO 13" LONG, THESE CINNAMON-BROWN BIRDS HAVE LONG, WHITE, MUSTACHE-LIKE STRIPES ON THEIR FACES THAT MAKE THEM LOOK LIKE LITTLE AVIAN MARK TWAINS (SEE FIGURE 29).

SIGNATURE BIRD SONG

KNOWN FOR A DISTINCTIVE 'WEEEEEEEE-TJAH' NOISE THAT SOUNDS EXACTLY LIKE A TODDLER PRACTICING KARATE.

PERFECT FOR INSULTING

- ☐ SHADY LUMBERJACKS
- ☐ SALVADOR DALÍ
- ☐ ANYONE IN PORTLAND

FUN FACT: THEY PROBE FOR FOOD IN THE CREVICES OF TREE BARK—LIKE DOLLY PARTON FINDING OLD POPCORN IN HER CLEAVAGE.

NATIVE AREAS

FOUND IN THE WOODLANDS OF BRAZIL—WHERE THEY, TOO, WOULD RATHER EATS BUGS THAN BRAZIL NUTS.

PREFER TO USE THE LATIN BINOMIAL NAME? YOU MAKE ME SICK TO MY XIPHOCOLAPTES FALCIROSTRIS.

FIG. 29
I'LL PASS, YOU MOUSTACHED WOODCREEPER.

LAY OFF THE SPRAY TAN, YOU ORANGE-CHEEKED WAXBILL.
FIG. 30

ORANGE-CHEEKED WAXBILL

AVERAGING ABOUT 4" LONG, THESE PRIMARILY BROWN AND GRAY BIRDS ARE KNOWN FOR THEIR VIBRANT ORANGE CHEEKS. ALSO KNOWN FOR ITS ORANGE CHEEKS? THAT MOUSE THAT ATE OUR BAG OF DORITOS LAST WINTER (SEE FIGURE 30).

SIGNATURE BIRD SONG

SOUNDS LIKE A SQUEAKY MATTRESS SPRING DURING AN ACTIVITY KNOWN FOR MAKING MATTRESS SPRINGS SQUEAK.

FUN FACT: THEY OFTEN EAT WHILE HANGING UPSIDE DOWN. THAT'S COOL—BUT CAN THEY EAT OREOS WHILE WEARING A SNUGGIE?

PERFECT FOR INSULTING

- CARROT AFICIONADOS ☐
- BABIES THAT HAVE JAUNDICE ☐
- NEMO ☐

NATIVE AREAS

FOUND IN AFRICA, JAPAN, SPAIN, HAWAII, AND PARTS OF THE CARIBBEAN. STILL NO WORD ON CARMEN SANDIEGO, THOUGH.

ESTRILDA MELPODA—THAT'S EITHER THE LATIN BINOMIAL NAME OR A 'HOT SINGLE IN YOUR AREA.'

THREE-WATTLED BELLBIRD

TYPICALLY 10 TO 12" LONG, WITH A WHITE HEAD AND SOLID CHESTNUT BODY. IF YOU SQUINT, IT KIND OF LOOKS LIKE A MINIATURE BALD EAGLE—IF SAID EAGLE WAS MIXED WITH A SOUL-SNATCHING DEMON SPAWN (SEE FIGURE 31).

SIGNATURE BIRD SONG

AN ALIEN-ESQUE, METALLIC 'EEH' SOUND THAT YOU'D HALF-EXPECT TO COME OUT OF MARK ZUCKERBERG'S MOUTH.

PERFECT FOR INSULTING

- [ ] GAME SHOW CONTESTANTS
- [ ] PEOPLE WITH THIRD NIPPLES
- [ ] AMATEUR CYCLISTS

FUN FACT: MALE BELLBIRDS PERCH AND DISPLAY THEIR WATTLES TO COURT FEMALES. WHEN HUMANS DO THIS, IT'S CALLED A 'FELONY.'

NATIVE AREAS

MAINLY FOUND IN CENTRAL AND SOUTH AMERICA. SO NOW WE KNOW WHERE THE PORTAL TO THE UNDERWORLD MUST BE.

PROCNIAS TRICARUNCULATUS—THAT'S EITHER THE LATIN BINOMIAL NAME OR WHAT WebMD SAYS THIS RASH IS.

FIG. 31

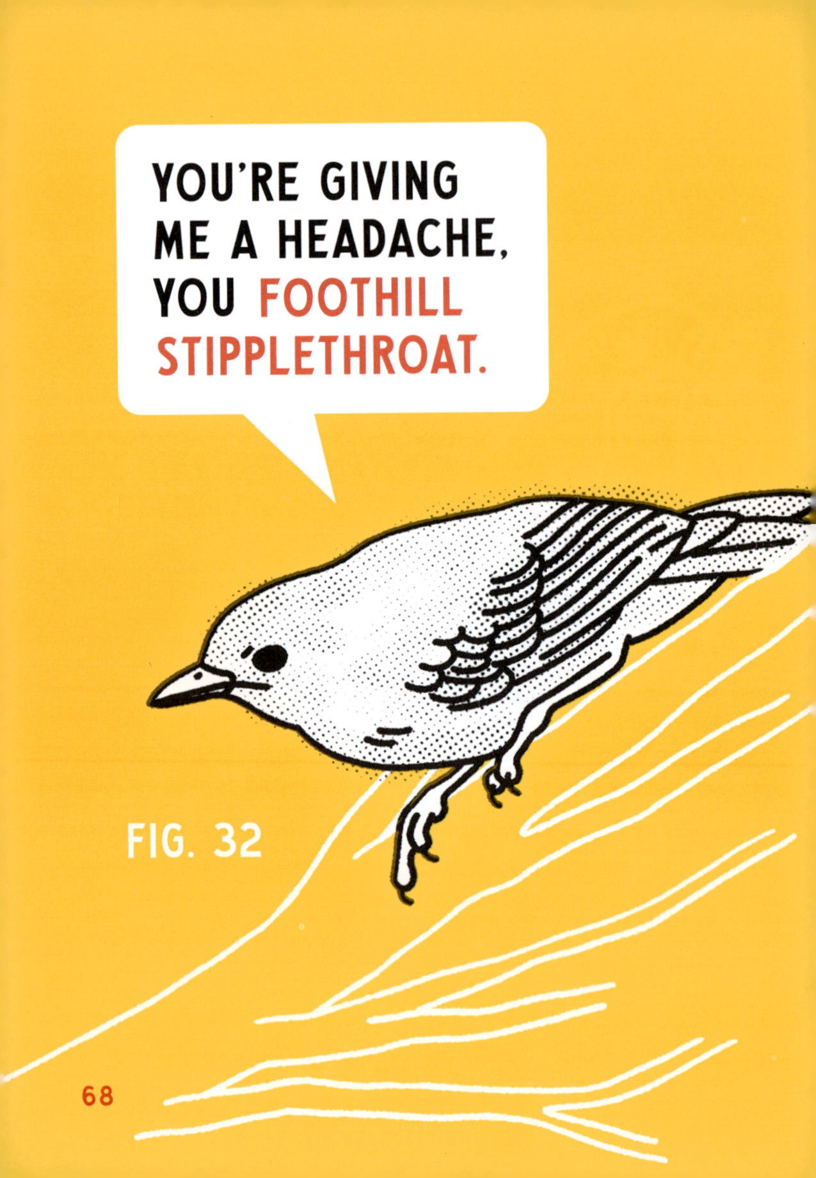

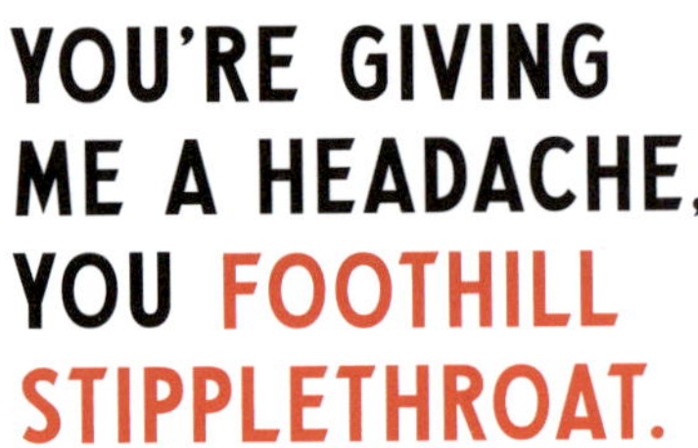

FIG. 32

FOOTHILL STIPPLETHROAT

ROUGHLY 4" LONG, THESE GRAYISH-BROWN BIRDS ARE BEST KNOWN FOR THE BLACK AND WHITE STIPPLED PATCH UNDER THEIR BEAKS. JUST PICTURE YOUR DAD WHEN HE DOESN'T SHAVE OVER THE HOLIDAYS (SEE FIGURE 32).

SIGNATURE BIRD SONG

A RISING AND FALLING SERIES OF HIGH-PITCHED NOTES, LIKE CHILDREN SCREAMING ON A REALLY BUMPY BUS RIDE.

FUN FACT: SCIENTISTS HAVE NOT YET BEEN ABLE TO OBSERVE THEIR BREEDING HABITS. THOSE CREEPS.

PERFECT FOR INSULTING

- NPR RADIO HOSTS ☐
- PEOPLE WITH NECK TATTOOS ☐
- MOONSHINE DRINKERS ☐

NATIVE AREAS

FOUND IN THE FOOTHILLS OF ECUADOR AND PERU—WHICH WOULD BE GREAT, IF THEY'D JUST GET AN IKEA.

OH, YOU PREFER TO USE THE LATIN BINOMIAL NAME? GAG ME WITH A SPOON, YOU EPINECROPHYLLA SPODIONOTA.

CALIFORNIA SCRUB JAY

APPROXIMATELY 11 TO 12" LONG, WITH A VIBRANT BLUE HEAD, WINGS, AND TAIL. THEY MAY LOOK LIKE BLUE JAYS, BUT TRUE TO THEIR WEST COAST ROOTS, THEY'RE FREQUENTLY SPOTTED AT DODGERS GAMES (SEE FIGURE 33).

SIGNATURE BIRD SONG

KNOWN FOR AN ELECTRONIC-ISH 'JAYY?' SQUAWK THAT SOUNDS LIKE EVERY SOUND EFFECT ON THE ATARI 2600.

PERFECT FOR INSULTING

- [ ] EREWHON SHOPPERS
- [ ] KNOCK-OFF SCRUB DADDIES
- [ ] DRIVERS ON THE 405

FUN FACT: THEY BURY SEEDS AND USE THEIR MEMORY TO FIND THEM MONTHS LATER—BUT SADLY, THEY FORGOT ABOUT THE ALAMO.

NATIVE AREAS

MAINLY FOUND IN CALIFORNIA, WHERE THEY ARE FIERCE DEFENDERS OF THEIR NESTS—AND IN-N-OUT BURGER.

APHELOCOMA CALIFORNICA—THAT'S EITHER THE LATIN BINOMIAL NAME OR AN OVERPRICED COCKTAIL.

TOUCH GRASS,
YOU CALIFORNIA
SCRUB JAY.
FIG. 33

WHERE ARE YOUR SHOES,
YOU LONG-TOED STINT?
FIG. 34

LONG-TOED STINT

TYPICALLY 5 TO 6" LONG, THESE SPECKLED BROWN AND WHITE BIRDS HAVE SUPER TINY HEADS WITH PALE STREAKS ABOVE THEIR EYES. THEY'RE ALSO THE ONLY BIRD THAT CAN SHARE SHOES WITH SHAQUILLE O'NEAL (SEE FIGURE 34).

SIGNATURE BIRD SONG

A SERIES OF 'PRRIT-PRRIT-PRRIT' NOISES—IDENTICAL TO A METAL DETECTOR WHEN YOU FIND A SWEET BOTTLE CAP.

FUN FACT: THEIR MIDDLE TOE IS OFTEN LONGER THAN THEIR BILL. CUT THEM OFF IN TRAFFIC AND THEY'LL SHOW IT TO YOU.

PERFECT FOR INSULTING

- CHRONIC SANDAL WEARERS ☐
- PEOPLE WITH MORTON'S TOE ☐
- E.T. ☐

NATIVE AREAS

THEY'RE QUITE THE WORLD TRAVELERS. SO HONESTLY, IF THERE'S A 'WETLAND,' THEY'VE PROBABLY BEEN TO IT.

CALIDRIS SUBMINUTA—THAT'S EITHER THE LATIN BINOMIAL NAME OR THE SPEED AT WHICH WE CAN EAT A TACO.

SOOTY BUSHTIT

AROUND 4" LONG, THESE MOSTLY BROWN BIRDS HAVE A GRAY HEAD AND A DISTINCT WHITE RING AROUND THEIR NECK—KIND OF LIKE THEY'RE WEARING ONE OF THOSE FAKE TURTLENECKS WITHOUT A SHIRT (SEE FIGURE 35).

SIGNATURE BIRD SONG

A SERIES OF MELODIC 'TWITTERINGS'—FOR WHICH THEY'VE REPORTEDLY RECEIVED A CEASE AND DESIST FROM DISNEY.

PERFECT FOR INSULTING

- [ ] GIRLS HITTING PUBERTY
- [ ] ANYONE AFTER YARD WORK
- [ ] GEORGE W. BUSH

FUN FACT: THEY ARE ALSO KNOWN AS THE WHITE-NECKLACED TIT—BUT MAYBE DON'T GOOGLE THAT ONE AT WORK. TRUST US.

NATIVE AREAS

FOUND IN THE TEMPERATE FORESTS OF CHINA—WHICH SOUNDS LIKE A WAY BETTER CHOICE THAN THE BOILING HOT ONES.

AEGITHALOS FULIGINOSUS—THAT'S EITHER THE LATIN BINOMIAL NAME OR A BUDGET GREEK GOD.

FIG. 35
MAYBE TRY SHOWERING, YOU SOOTY BUSHTIT.

WHAT A THEORY, YOU
GREAT LIZARD-CUCKOO.
FIG. 36

GREAT LIZARD-CUCKOO

RANGING FROM 16 TO 21" LONG, THESE GIANT OLIVE-BROWN MONSTERS HAVE LIGHT-COLORED THROATS AND SUSPICIOUSLY RED EYES THAT THEY ALWAYS BLAME ON THEIR ALLERGIES—DESPITE BEING HUGE BOB MARLEY FANS (SEE FIGURE 36).

SIGNATURE BIRD SONG

A CACKLING 'KA-KA-KA' SOUND, LIKE AN EVIL WITCH THAT IS PROBABLY JUST LONELY AND MISUNDERSTOOD.

FUN FACT: THEY ENJOY EATING LIZARDS—SPOILER ALERT FOR THE SERIES FINALE OF THOSE 'GEICO' COMMERCIALS.

PERFECT FOR INSULTING

- FLAT-EARTHERS ☐
- HERPETOLOGY PROFESSORS ☐
- CROCODILE DUNDEE ☐

NATIVE AREAS

THEY PRIMARILY LIVE IN THE FORESTS OF CUBA AND THE BAHAMAS—WHICH EXPLAINS WHY THEY CAN'T FIND ANY VISINE.

OH, YOU PREFER TO USE THE LATIN BINOMIAL NAME? I HOPE YOU SPRAIN YOUR COCCYZUS MERLINI.

CEBU BOOBOOK

TYPICALLY 10" LONG, WITH BROWN AND WHITE PATTERNING ALL OVER THEIR BODY. BUT HONESTLY, IT'S THEIR PIERCING YELLOW EYES THAT ARE THE REAL STAR. AND BY 'STAR,' WE MEAN 'EXTREMELY TERRIFYING' (SEE FIGURE 37).

SIGNATURE BIRD SONG

A SOFT 'WHOOP-WHOOP' NOISE, LIKE AN UNENTHUSIASTIC AUDIENCE MEMBER OF 'THE ARSENIO HALL SHOW.'

PERFECT FOR INSULTING

- [ ] RUDE LIBRARIANS
- [ ] THE 'READING RAINBOW' GUY
- [ ] BOO RADLEY

FUN FACT: THEY DON'T HAVE EARS, WHICH WILL COME IN HANDY IF KATY PERRY EVER DECIDES TO TOUR IN THE PHILIPPINES.

NATIVE AREAS

EXCLUSIVELY FOUND ON THE ISLAND OF CEBU—BUT IF THERE WAS A 'BRASS MONKEY' ISLAND, WE WOULDN'T LEAVE EITHER.

NINOX RUMSEYI—THAT'S EITHER THE LATIN BINOMIAL NAME OR SOME CELEBRITY'S ATTEMPT AT A BABY NAME.

SHOVE IT UP YOUR CEBU BOOBOOK.
FIG. 37

FIG. 38

ZIGZAG HERON

APPROXIMATELY 11 TO 14" LONG, THESE DARK GRAY BIRDS ARE COVERED IN A WAVY PATTERN THAT'S REMINISCENT OF THE STATIC ON OFF-CHANNEL TUBE TVs. WE THINK. WE'RE FAR TOO YOUNG TO KNOW ANYTHING ABOUT THAT (SEE FIGURE 38).

SIGNATURE BIRD SONG

YOU KNOW THAT TIME YOUR BROTHER SUCKER PUNCHED YOU IN THE STOMACH? WELL, YOU MADE THE SAME 'OOOP' SOUND.

FUN FACT: THEY ARE NOTORIOUSLY RECLUSIVE—BUT THEY'LL HANG OUT WITH YOU IF YOU GUILT THEM HARD ENOUGH.

PERFECT FOR INSULTING

- PUB CRAWL PARTICIPANTS ☐
- OVERLY CONFIDENT HIKERS ☐
- MID-2000s LINDSAY LOHAN ☐

NATIVE AREAS

OFTEN FOUND IN THE SWAMPS OF BRAZIL AND NEIGHBORING COUNTRIES. SO THEY REALLY LOVE THE TROPICS, OR COCAINE.

OH, YOU PREFER TO USE THE LATIN BINOMIAL NAME? WHO PUT A STICK UP YOUR ZEBRILUS UNDULATUS?

LONG-TAILED GROUND ROLLER

TYPICALLY AROUND 13 TO 18" LONG, THESE BROWN AND WHITE BIRDS HAVE BLUE TIPPED WINGS AND SHOCKINGLY LONG TAILS. KIND OF LIKE A CERTAIN WILLEM DAFOE APPENDAGE, IF THOSE RUMORS ARE TO BE BELIEVED (SEE FIGURE 39).

SIGNATURE BIRD SONG

KNOWN FOR A SHORT, REPETITIVE 'TUC' NOISE THAT SOUNDS ALMOST IDENTICAL TO MARIO JUMPING.

PERFECT FOR INSULTING

- ☐ MEN WITH PONYTAILS
- ☐ YOUR NEIGHBOR'S DOG
- ☐ LIEUTENANT DAN

FUN FACT: DURING COURTSHIP, THE MALES FEED THE FEMALES, WHICH IS LIKELY THE MOST ROMANTIC WAY AN EARTHWORM HAS EVER BEEN EATEN.

NATIVE AREAS

DESPITE LIVING EXCLUSIVELY IN A VERY SMALL SECTION OF MADAGASCAR'S SPINY FOREST, THEY ARE NOTORIOUSLY SHY AND HARD TO LOCATE. REGARDLESS, A FEW OF THEM ARE STILL REALLY PISSED ABOUT NOT BEING IN THAT 2005 DREAMWORKS FILM.

WHAT'S THAT SMELL, YOU LONG-TAILED GROUND ROLLER?

FIG. 39

FIG. 40

RED-FACED WARBLER

ABOUT 5 TO 6" LONG, WITH AN ASH-GRAY BODY THAT YOU'LL HARDLY NOTICE—MAINLY BECAUSE THEIR FIRE-ENGINE-RED FACE AND BLACK TOUPEE-LIKE HEAD PATCH MAKE THEM LOOK LIKE A SUN-BURNT USED CAR SALESMAN (SEE FIGURE 40).

SIGNATURE BIRD SONG

A DELIGHTFUL 'SWEET-SWEET-SWEET-WEETA-SEE-SEE-SEE' MELODY THAT SETS UNREALISTIC STANDARDS FOR OTHER BIRDS.

FUN FACT: THEIR FACES STAY THE SAME VIVID RED COLOR ALL YEAR. YOU KNOW, JUST LIKE SANTA CLAUS—AND ALCOHOLICS.

PERFECT FOR INSULTING

- UV LIGHT SKEPTICS ☐
- KIDS THROWING TANTRUMS ☐
- THE KOOL-AID MAN ☐

NATIVE AREAS

MOSTLY FOUND IN MEXICO, BUT THEY'LL OCCASIONALLY FLY TO THE SOUTHERN U.S. TO FIND THAT SPECIAL SOMEBODY.

CARDELLINA RUBRIFRONS—THAT'S EITHER THE LATIN BINOMIAL NAME OR THE PRESIDENT OF A TERRIBLE HOA.

THICK-BILLED GROUND PIGEON

ROUGHLY 11 TO 12" LONG, THESE BIRDS ARE MOSTLY A DARK BLUEISH-GRAY WITH A LIGHT PEACH BOTTOM THAT MAKES IT LOOK LIKE THEY DON'T HAVE ANY PANTS ON. WHICH THEY DON'T. LISTEN, YOU KNOW WHAT WE MEAN (SEE FIGURE 41).

SIGNATURE BIRD SONG

A BUNCH OF LOW, REPETITIVE 'HOO' SOUNDS—LIKE A NEWLY FORMED JUG BAND TRYING TO REHEARSE.

PERFECT FOR INSULTING

- ☐ IRS AUDITORS
- ☐ CELEBRITIES WITH LIP FILLER
- ☐ ANYONE UNDER 5' 4"

FUN FACT: THE MALES SIT ON THE EGG DURING THE DAY—WHICH MAY OR MAY NOT HAVE INSPIRED THE 1983 FILM 'MR. MOM.'

NATIVE AREAS

EXCLUSIVELY FOUND ON THE ISLAND OF NEW GUINEA—BECAUSE WHILE THEY ARE CAPABLE OF FLIGHT, IT'S NOT REALLY THEIR THING. THEY'D MOSTLY PREFER TO JUST WALK AROUND AND EAT SEEDS AND STUFF. SAME HERE—EXCEPT WITH SITTING AND A BOX OF WINE.

HOW OBSERVANT, YOU THICK-BILLED GROUND PIGEON.

FIG. 41

LEARN TO DRIVE, YOU WRINKLED HORNBILL.
FIG. 42

WRINKLED HORNBILL

TYPICALLY 25 TO 28" LONG, THIS LARGE BIRD IS KNOWN FOR HAVING A BLACK BODY, A YELLOW NECK, AND A LINGERING INFERIORITY COMPLEX ABOUT THE SIZABLE GROWTH ON TOP OF ITS GIANT BEAK (SEE FIGURE 42).

SIGNATURE BIRD SONG

A MONOTONE 'HA-HA-HA' NOISE THAT SOUNDS LIKE YOUR MOM PRETENDING TO LAUGH AT A JOKE SHE DOESN'T GET.

FUN FACT: THEY NEVER DRINK WATER—ALL THEIR MOISTURE COMES FROM FOOD. FINALLY, WE'VE FOUND OUR TRUE SPIRIT ANIMAL.

PERFECT FOR INSULTING

- RUDE SENIOR CITIZENS ☐
- LEISURELY BATH-TAKERS ☐
- GÉRARD DEPARDIEU ☐

NATIVE AREAS

FOUND IN THE FORESTS OF SUMATRA, BORNEO, AND SOME OTHER PLACES THAT ALSO SOUND LIKE THEY WOULD BE HUMID.

RHABDOTORRHINUS CORRUGATUS—THAT'S EITHER THE LATIN BINOMIAL NAME OR ONE OF THOSE LAWSUIT ILLNESSES.

BLUE-CAPPED PUFFLEG

USUALLY 4 TO 5" LONG, WITH IRIDESCENT COLORING ON ITS HEAD AND BODY, THIS BIRD FEATURES BUILT-IN WHITE LEGWARMERS THAT WOULD FIT RIGHT IN AT ANY RESPECTABLE JAZZERCISE CLASS IN THE 1980s (SEE FIGURE 43).

SIGNATURE BIRD SONG

A QUIET, PATHETIC LITTLE 'ZEE-ZEE.' HONESTLY, IT JUST SOUNDS LIKE THEY'VE GIVEN UP ON LIFE.

PERFECT FOR INSULTING

- [ ] PEOPLE WITH JNCO JEANS
- [ ] TRAIN CONDUCTORS
- [ ] THE PILLSBURY DOUGHBOY

FUN FACT: THEY PREFER TO LIVE IN HUMID CLIMATES—SO IF THEY ARE EVER LOOKING TO RELOCATE, KANSAS CITY WOULD BE PERFECT.

NATIVE AREAS

THEY PRIMARILY LIVE ON THE EASTERN SLOPE OF THE ANDES MOUNTAINS. THE WESTERN SLOPE? THAT'S FOR LOSERS.

PREFER TO USE THE LATIN BINOMIAL NAME? YOU GIVE ME THE CREEPS, YOU ERIOCNEMIS GLAUCOPOIDES.

FIG. 43
PICK UP THE PACE, YOU BLUE-CAPPED PUFFLEG.

HOW WERE THE DORITOS, YOU RED-WHISKERED BULBUL?
FIG. 44

RED-WHISKERED BULBUL

ROUGHLY 8" LONG, THIS BIRD IS KNOWN FOR ITS TALL BLACK CREST AND RED CHEEK PATCHES. IF WES ANDERSON MADE A STOP-MOTION, BIRD-BASED 'LITTLE RASCALS' MOVIE, THIS THING WOULD BE A SHOO-IN FOR ALFALFA (SEE FIGURE 44).

SIGNATURE BIRD SONG

A SERIES OF HIGH-PITCHED 'PIK-PIK-A-WEW' NOISES THAT MIGHT AS WELL JUST BE GIZMO OUTTAKES FROM 'GREMLINS.'

FUN FACT: THEY CAN CONSUME SOME POISONOUS PLANTS—JUST LIKE US TACKLING THAT BLOCK OF CHEESE THANKS TO LACTAID.

PERFECT FOR INSULTING

- ANYONE EATING SPAGHETTI ☐
- REDHEADS HITTING PUBERTY ☐
- YUKON CORNELIUS ☐

NATIVE AREAS

MAINLY FOUND IN TROPICAL ASIA—BUT THEY'VE ALSO FOUND HOMES IN FLORIDA, HAWAII, AND MOST NOTABLY, OUR HEARTS.

PYCNONOTUS JOCOSUS—THAT'S EITHER THE LATIN BINOMIAL NAME OR SOME 17-YEAR-OLD'S FAKE ID NAME.

YELLOW-BELLIED FLOWERPECKER

ABOUT 5" LONG, THIS BIRD HAS A DISTINCTIVE WHITE STRIPE DOWN ITS NECK THAT MAKES IT LOOK LIKE IT'S WEARING A TINY GRAY JACKET WITH BRIGHT YELLOW PANTS. IN OTHER WORDS, THIS BIRD IS HARRY STYLES (SEE FIGURE 45).

SIGNATURE BIRD SONG

YOU KNOW THAT ONE BAD SHOPPING CART WITH THE STUCK, SQUEAKY WHEEL THAT YOU ALWAYS GET? IT'S LIKE THAT.

PERFECT FOR INSULTING

- [ ] BOTANICAL GARDENERS
- [ ] PUBLIC PARK FLASHERS
- [ ] THE YELLOW CARE BEAR

FUN FACT: THEY REALLY ENJOY MISTLETOE. EATING IT—NOT HANGING OUT UNDER IT LIKE THAT CREEP AT THE OFFICE HOLIDAY PARTY.

NATIVE AREAS

OFTEN FOUND IN AND AROUND THE FORESTS OF THE HIMALAYAS—WHERE, HONESTLY, THEY ARE JUST GETTING REALLY SICK OF HEARING ABOUT THAT PINK SALT. BUT THEN AGAIN, AREN'T WE ALL?

FIG. 45

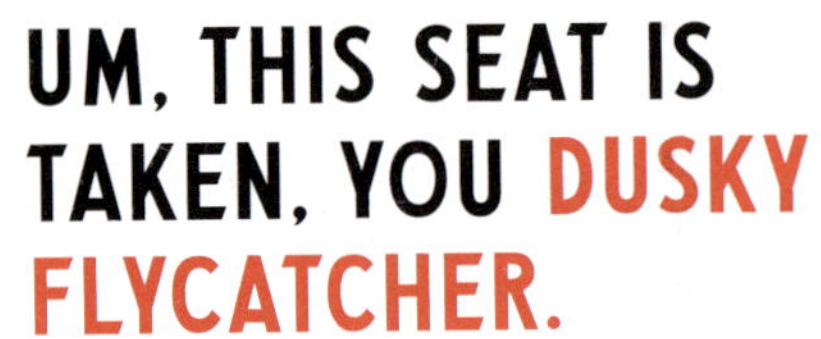

FIG. 46

DUSKY FLYCATCHER

TYPICALLY 5" LONG, WITH AN OLIVE-COLORED BACK AND GREY HEAD, THIS BIRD IS KNOWN TO HAVE A SUBTLE TEARDROP-SHAPED EYE-RING THAT MAY OR MAY NOT MEAN THAT THEY KILLED A GUY IN PRISON (SEE FIGURE 46).

SIGNATURE BIRD SONG

A QUICK, HIGH-PITCHED 'BEAN-DIP' NOISE—JUST LIKE US, THE MOMENT WE SET FOOT INSIDE OF A TEX-MEX RESTAURANT.

FUN FACT: THEY ARE KNOWN TO WHACK PREY AGAINST BRANCHES TO SUBDUE IT—LIKE WHEN YOU OPEN THOSE PILLSBURY TUBES.

PERFECT FOR INSULTING

- INFREQUENT BATHERS ☐
- OPEN MOUTH BREATHERS ☐
- MR. MIYAGI ☐

NATIVE AREAS

MIGRATES TO THE WESTERN U.S. TO BREED—AND PROBABLY WAIT TABLES WHILE THEY AUDITION FOR COMMERCIALS.

EMPIDONAX OBERHOLSERI—THAT'S EITHER THE LATIN BINOMIAL NAME OR A STYLE OF PANTS SOLD IN GERMANY.

FORK-TAILED WOODNYMPH

USUALLY JUST 3 TO 5" LONG, WITH GLITTERING, IRIDESCENT GREEN AND BLUE PLUMAGE, AND UNDERSTATED BLACK BILLS. THESE BIRDS WOULD DEFINITELY BEAT ELTON JOHN IN A 'WHO WORE IT BETTER?' MATCHUP (SEE FIGURE 47).

SIGNATURE BIRD SONG

IMAGINE THE 'SEE-TSEET' SOUND YOU HEAR WHEN YOU NEED TO REPLACE THE SMOKE ALARM BATTERIES. REPEATEDLY.

PERFECT FOR INSULTING

- [ ] BOY SCOUT LEADERS
- [ ] ORCHESTRA CONDUCTORS
- [ ] MR. BELVEDERE

FUN FACT: MALES ARE KNOWN TO AGGRESSIVELY DEFEND PATCHES OF FLOWERS—MUCH IN THE WAY WE PROTECT OUR CURLY FRIES.

NATIVE AREAS

FOUND IN EVERY MAINLAND SOUTH AMERICAN COUNTRY EXCEPT CHILE AND URUGUAY—THEY'RE JUST TOO TOURISTY.

THALURANIA FURCATA—THAT'S EITHER THE LATIN BINOMIAL NAME OR AN EXTRA IN THE 'CATS' MUSICAL.

FIG. 47

DID YOU FART, YOU SWAMP PALM BULBUL?
FIG. 48

SWAMP PALM BULBUL

ROUGHLY 9" LONG, THESE MOSTLY BROWN BIRDS ARE NOTABLE FOR THE TINY WHITE-TIPPED FEATHERS THAT GIVE THEIR FACES A SCALY, GRIZZLED APPEARANCE—LIKE THE BROODING LOVE INTEREST IN A ROMANTASY NOVEL (SEE FIGURE 48).

SIGNATURE BIRD SONG

A SERIES OF CACKLES THAT SOUND ALMOST HUMAN—IF THAT HUMAN WERE ALVIN FROM 'ALVIN AND THE CHIPMUNKS.'

FUN FACT: MALES AND FEMALES HAVE NO EXTERNAL DIFFERENCES IN APPEARANCE—AS IF DATING WASN'T HARD ENOUGH ALREADY.

PERFECT FOR INSULTING

- CLAMMY HANDSHAKERS ☐
- CHRONIC STEAM ROOM USERS ☐
- SHREK LOOK-ALIKES ☐

NATIVE AREAS

PRIMARILY FOUND IN WET, SWAMPY FORESTS AROUND THE CONGO—WHERE MANY STILL BRAG ABOUT MEETING TIM CURRY.

OH, YOU PREFER TO USE THE LATIN BINOMIAL NAME? SOUNDS LIKE YOU CAUGHT THESCELOCICHLA LEUCOPLEURA.

BLUE-BEARDED BEE-EATER

TYPICALLY 12 TO 14" LONG, WITH BLUISH-GREEN PLUMAGE, THESE BIRDS ARE KNOWN FOR THEIR HIGHLY REFINED TASTE IN INSECTS—WHICH IS ALSO WHY THE RAW HONEY COMMUNITY IS ALWAYS ON THEIR ASS (SEE FIGURE 49).

SIGNATURE BIRD SONG

RAPID 'UHN-UHN-UHNA' SOUNDS, LIKE AN AIRPORT METAL DETECTOR CIRCLING THAT BELT YOU FORGOT TO TAKE OFF.

PERFECT FOR INSULTING

- [ ] SMURF COSPLAYERS
- [ ] KIDS AT A BLUEBERRY PATCH
- [ ] THE BOY IN 'MY GIRL'

FUN FACT: THEY AREN'T VERY GRACEFUL FLIERS. IT'S OKAY, WE AREN'T EITHER—UNLESS WE'VE HAD A XANAX.

NATIVE AREAS

FOUND IN MUCH OF INDIA AND PARTS OF SOUTHEAST ASIA—BUT NOT BY US. WE WENT TO CANADA ONCE, THOUGH.

NYCTYORNIS ATHERTONI—THAT'S EITHER THE LATIN BINOMIAL NAME OR SOME TYPE OF MEDICAL SPAGHETTI.

FIG. 49
UM, THAT'S NOT EDIBLE, YOU BLUE-BEARDED BEE-EATER.

YOUR VOICE COULD CURE INSOMNIA, YOU MONOTONOUS LARK.

FIG. 50

MONOTONOUS LARK

APPROXIMATELY 14" LONG, WITH DISTINCTIVE BROWN AND WHITE PLUMAGE AND A SEMI-SPIKY HAIRDO ON TOP. HONESTLY, JUST PICTURE GUY FIERI—BUT WITHOUT THE GOATEE AND FLAME-COVERED SHIRT, UNFORTUNATELY (SEE FIGURE 50).

SIGNATURE BIRD SONG

DESPITE NOT BEING OLD-TIMEY BRITISH ORPHANS, THESE BIRDS GO AROUND CHIRPING 'FOR-SYRUP-IS-SWEET' ALL DAY LONG.

FUN FACT: THEY APPEAR IN LARGE NUMBERS AFTER HEAVY RAINS TO BREED. WHICH IS KIND OF WHAT HAPPENED AT WOODSTOCK, TOO.

PERFECT FOR INSULTING

- ACTORS IN HR VIDEOS ☐
- STAMP COLLECTORS ☐
- YOUR OLD HISTORY TEACHER ☐

NATIVE AREAS

SPREAD ACROSS SIX COUNTRIES IN SOUTHERN AFRICA, WHERE THEIR FAVORITE PASTIME IS POOPING ON SAFARI TOURS.

MIRAFRA PASSERINA—THAT'S EITHER THE LATIN BINOMIAL NAME OR SOME LADY RUNNING FOR CITY COUNCIL.

LOGGERHEAD SHRIKE

ROUGHLY 8 TO 10" LONG, WITH A GRAY AND WHITE BODY, AND A BLACK MASK-LIKE STREAK ACROSS THEIR EYES THAT SCREAMS 'HI-YO, SILVER!'—WHICH IS A GREAT REFERENCE FOR ANYONE READING THAT'S 112 YEARS OLD (SEE FIGURE 51).

SIGNATURE BIRD SONG

AN ENDLESSLY REPETITIVE 'TCHEEK-TCHEEK' SOUND—LIKE YOUR TURN SIGNAL AT A REALLY LONG RED LIGHT.

PERFECT FOR INSULTING

- [ ] CHAINSAW ARTISTS
- [ ] TO-DO LIST ENTHUSIASTS
- [ ] THE BRAWNY MAN

FUN FACT: THEY LIKE TO KILL THEIR PREY BY IMPALING IT ON THORNS OR BARBED WIRE. SO FUN.

NATIVE AREAS

THEY PRIMARILY LIVE IN THE SOUTHERN U.S. AND MEXICO, BUT MIGRATE TO CANADA FOR BREEDING—AND PANCAKES.

PREFER TO USE THE LATIN BINOMIAL NAME? WELL, YOU CAN SHOVE IT RIGHT UP YOUR LANIUS LUDOVICIANUS.

FIG. 51

OK. I'LL SAY IT SLOWER, YOU STRAW-HEADED BULBUL.
FIG. 52

STRAW-HEADED BULBUL

AVERAGING 11" LONG, WITH BROWN AND OLIVE PLUMAGE. WELL, ALL EXCEPT FOR THEIR AWKWARDLY BLEACH-BLONDE HEADS THAT LOOK LIKE A DIVORCED DAD GOING THROUGH A BIT OF A MIDLIFE CRISIS (SEE FIGURE 52).

SIGNATURE BIRD SONG

A SERIES OF FUTURISTIC, WHIRLY CHIRPS—LIKE APOCALYPTIC ROBOTS CALCULATING THE VALUE OF YOUR EXISTENCE.

FUN FACT: DUE TO THEIR BEAUTIFUL SINGING VOICES, THEY'RE OFTEN HELD CAPTIVE TO ENTERTAIN OTHERS—JUST LIKE THE JACKSONS WERE.

PERFECT FOR INSULTING

- CORNFIELD SCARECROWS ☐
- JIMMY BUFFETT FANS ☐
- JUSTIN TIMBERLAKE IN 1999 ☐

NATIVE AREAS

CAN BE SEEN FLOURISHING IN SINGAPORE, WHERE THEY'RE A PROTECTED SPECIES—AND FINALLY FINDING THEMSELVES.

OH, YOU PREFER TO USE THE LATIN BINOMIAL NAME? GET A LOAD OF THIS PYCNONOTUS ZEYLANICUS.

BUFF-RUMPED THORNBILL

APPROXIMATELY 4" IN LENGTH, THESE BIRDS HAVE GRAYISH BACKS, GREENISH BELLIES, AND THE SORT OF BUILD WHERE YOU CAN'T QUITE TELL WHERE THEIR NECKS END AND THEIR BODIES BEGIN—LIKE YOUR OLD LANDLORD (SEE FIGURE 53).

SIGNATURE BIRD SONG

A HIGH, RAPID 'PITTA-PITTA-PITTA-PIT' NOISE—MUCH LIKE HOW BIRD-SIZED JACKHAMMERS WOULD SOUND IF THEY EXISTED.

PERFECT FOR INSULTING

- ☐ RUDE PERSONAL TRAINERS
- ☐ WRANGLER JEAN MODELS
- ☐ THAT GUY FROM 'ROXANNE'

FUN FACT: A FEMALE BIRD WILL GET UP TO THREE MALES TO HELP HER BUILD A NEST—BEFORE TELLING THEM THEY'RE LIKE BROTHERS TO HER.

NATIVE AREAS

EXCLUSIVELY FOUND IN THE WOODLANDS OF EASTERN AUSTRALIA, WHERE EVERY DAY IS A LEG DAY.

ACANTHIZA REGULOIDES—THAT'S EITHER THE LATIN BINOMIAL NAME OR A LAXATIVE FOR WITCHES.

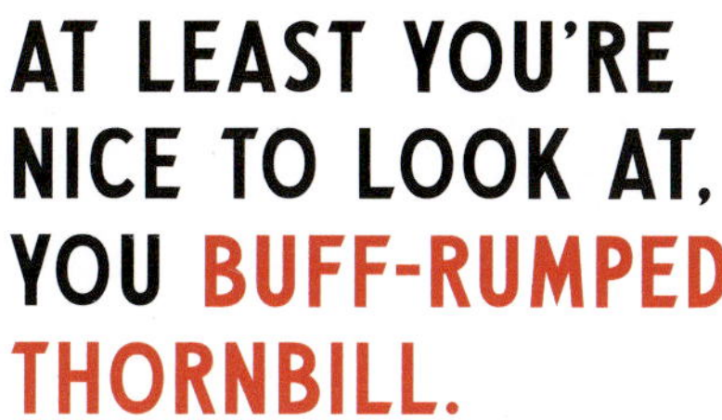

FIG. 53

THAT'S QUITE A SMILE, YOU TOOTH-BILLED BOWERBIRD.
FIG. 54

TOOTH-BILLED BOWERBIRD

USUALLY 11" LONG, THESE BROWN BIRDS ARE DISTINCTIVE FOR THEIR MOTTLED PLUMAGE AND SHORT, SERRATED BILLS. ESSENTIALLY, THEY LOOK A LOT LIKE A TRAVEL-SIZED VERSION OF A HAWK (SEE FIGURE 54).

SIGNATURE BIRD SONG

LOUD, HIGH-PITCHED SQUEALS THAT SOUND LIKE YOUR DOG WHEN YOU ACCIDENTALLY STEP ON ITS PAW, YOU JERK.

FUN FACT: DURING BREEDING, MALES CLEAR BITS OF RAINFOREST FLOOR TO DECORATE WITH LEAVES—WHICH IS BETTER THAN 'STAR WARS' POSTERS.

PERFECT FOR INSULTING

- PEOPLE WITH VENEERS ☐
- TRADER JOE'S CASHIERS ☐
- GARY BUSEY ☐

NATIVE AREAS

ONLY FOUND IN THE QUEENSLAND REGION OF AUSTRALIA. THEY WOULD TRAVEL, BUT THE JET LAG IS A REAL KILLER.

SCENOPOEETES DENTIROSTRIS—THAT'S EITHER THE LATIN BINOMIAL NAME OR MEDICAL-GRADE BAD BREATH.

RUFOUS-RUMPED SEEDEATER

TYPICALLY 9.5" LONG, WITH MOSTLY GRAYISH-BLUE HEADS AND WINGS. ALTHOUGH, THANKS TO THEIR UNEXPECTEDLY BRIGHT ORANGE UNDERBELLIES, THEY JUST LOOK LIKE THEY SAT IN A BOWL OF CHILI (SEE FIGURE 55).

SIGNATURE BIRD SONG

A RAPID-FIRE SERIES OF VARIOUS CHIRPS THAT JUST SOUND LIKE A BUNCH OF FIREWORKS BEING SET OFF AT ONCE.

PERFECT FOR INSULTING

- ☐ OCCASIONAL VEGANS
- ☐ PRO BASEBALL PLAYERS
- ☐ SIR MIX-A-LOT'S MUSE

FUN FACT: VERY LITTLE IS KNOWN ABOUT THIS MYSTERIOUS LITTLE SEEDEATER—WHICH IS PRETTY MUCH WHAT THEY SAY ABOUT SIA, TOO.

NATIVE AREAS

FOUND IN THE TALL GRASSES OF SOUTH-CENTRAL SOUTH AMERICA—MAYBE TOWARDS THE NORTHEAST SIDE.

SPOROPHILA HYPOCHROMA—THAT'S EITHER THE LATIN BINOMIAL NAME OR THE MOLD GROWING IN OUR FRIDGE.

FIG. 55
UM, THEY DON'T ACTUALLY MILK ALMONDS, YOU RUFOUS-RUMPED SEEDEATER.

WAY TO RUIN THE MOOD, YOU KILLDEER.
FIG. 56

KILLDEER

ABOUT 8.5 TO 11" LONG, THIS OTHERWISE TYPICAL-LOOKING BIRD HAS SEVERAL BOLD BLACK STRIPES ACROSS ITS FACE AND NECK THAT SAYS: 'I HAVE A FREELANCE MIME GIG AT 2, BUT A WORK THING AT 3' (SEE FIGURE 56).

SIGNATURE BIRD SONG

A CONSTANT, HIGH-PITCHED 'KILL-DEER' CHANT, LIKE SOME PSYCHOTIC 6-YEAR-OLD GIRL THAT HATES WILDLIFE.

FUN FACT: THEY'VE SHOWN TO BE VERY TOLERANT OF HUMANS—WHICH, HONESTLY, IS WAY MORE THAN WE COULD SAY ABOUT OURSELVES.

PERFECT FOR INSULTING

- SEMITRUCK DRIVERS ☐
- VENISON CONNOISSEURS ☐
- THE WRITER OF 'BAMBI' ☐

NATIVE AREAS

COMMONLY FOUND ALL ACROSS NORTH AMERICA, OFTEN NEAR SHORE LINES—BUT THEY LIKE A GOOD PARKING LOT, TOO.

CHARADRIUS VOCIFERUS—THAT'S EITHER THE LATIN BINOMIAL NAME OR A GUY NAMED CHAD'S RENAISSANCE FAIRE ALIAS.

UNADORNED FLYCATCHER

ROUGHLY 4 TO 5" LONG, THESE BIRDS FEATURE DULL GREENISH BODIES AND CINNAMON-COLORED WINGS—AND ARE SO FLUFFY AND ROUND, THEY COULD EASILY BE MISTAKEN FOR THE FUR YOU BALL UP WHILE DE-SHEDDING YOUR DOG (SEE FIGURE 57).

SIGNATURE BIRD SONG

JUST IMAGINE AN ASSORTMENT OF TWEETS AND CHIRPS BEING INTERRUPTED BY AN OLD-TIMEY TELEPHONE RINGING.

PERFECT FOR INSULTING

- [ ] NAKED HITCHHIKERS
- [ ] BORING EXTERMINATORS
- [ ] JEFF GOLDBLUM

FUN FACT: THEY'RE WAY PRETTIER THAN THEIR NAME WOULD LEAD YOU TO BELIEVE—AND LIKELY NAMED BY AN UNADORNED JERK-FACE.

NATIVE AREAS

EXCLUSIVELY FOUND IN PARTS OF SOUTHERN PERU AND WESTERN BOLIVIA. THEY DON'T GET OUT MUCH.

PREFER TO USE THE LATIN BINOMIAL NAME? YOU CAN BE SUCH A PAIN IN THE MYIOPHOBUS INORNATUS.

FIG. 57

AS LONG AS YOU'RE HAPPY, BUFFLEHEAD.
FIG. 58

BUFFLEHEAD

APPROXIMATELY 10 TO 11" LONG, THIS MOSTLY BLACK AND WHITE DUCK IS DISTINCTIVE FOR ITS SHINY, GREENISH-PURPLE HEAD—AND ITS BIG WHITE PATCH THAT'S ROUGHLY THE SHAPE OF LARRY DAVID'S HAIRLINE (SEE FIGURE 58).

SIGNATURE BIRD SONG

A HALF-QUACK, HALF-BARK THAT'S ODDLY REMINISCENT OF A FIVE-POUND DOG TRYING TO DEFEND YOU FROM THE VACUUM.

FUN FACT: THEY CAN DIVE NEARLY 15 FEET DEEP FOR FOOD—WHICH IS A LOT LIKE WHEN WE HAD TO GET THAT CHEETO FROM UNDER THE COUCH.

PERFECT FOR INSULTING

- PEOPLE WITH MULLETS ☐
- CONSTANT HEAD NODDERS ☐
- JAY LENO ☐

NATIVE AREAS

THEY FLY TO THE SOUTHERN U.S. IN THE WINTER, WHERE THEY BLEND IN WITH THE TOURISTS BY LEAVING THEIR BLINKERS ON.

BUCEPHALA ALBEOLA—THAT'S EITHER THE LATIN BINOMIAL NAME OR ONE OF OUR GREAT-GREAT AUNTS.

DULL-COLORED GRASSQUIT

AROUND 4" LONG, THESE EXTRAORDINARILY MUNDANE BIRDS ARE A MUTED BROWN AND DEVOID OF ANY DISTINCTIVE MARKINGS. IF THEY WERE MONKS, THEY WOULD BE WINNING AT THAT WHOLE DESTITUTION THING (SEE FIGURE 59).

SIGNATURE BIRD SONG

A SQUEAKY 'ZEETIG-ZEEZEEZIG' NOISE—LIKE SOMEONE USING A SWING THAT REALLY NEEDS SOME WD-40.

PERFECT FOR INSULTING

- [ ] L.L. BEAN SHOPPERS
- [ ] APARTMENT PAINTERS
- [ ] WILLIE NELSON

FUN FACT: THEY HAVE SMALL HEADS AND LARGE REAR ENDS, JUST LIKE KIM KARDASHIAN—BUT LET'S NOT GIVE THESE BIRDS ANY IDEAS.

NATIVE AREAS

CAN BE FOUND, AND THEN QUICKLY FORGOTTEN ABOUT, IN THE ANDEAN FOOTHILLS OF SOUTH AMERICA.

OH, YOU PREFER TO USE THE LATIN BINOMIAL NAME? YOU DON'T EVEN EXIST TO ME, YOU ASEMOSPIZA OBSCURA.

FIG. 59

FIG. 60
GET A LOZENGE, YOU COMMON YELLOWTHROAT.

COMMON YELLOWTHROAT

ROUGHLY 5" LONG, THESE BIRDS HAVE GREENISH WINGS AND YELLOW NECKS—BUT IT'S THEIR BLACK, MASK-LIKE PATCHES THAT MAKE THEM EASY TO SPOT. JUST LIKE THOSE BUILDINGS THAT CLEARLY USED TO BE A PIZZA HUT (SEE FIGURE 60).

SIGNATURE BIRD SONG

A LOUD 'WICHETY-WICHETY-WICHETY' CHANT—SIMILAR TO WHAT SALEM, MASSACHUSETTS PROBABLY SOUNDED LIKE IN 1692.

FUN FACT: FOUND IN 1766, IT'S ONE OF THE FIRST BIRDS TO BE CATALOGED IN THE NEW WORLD—AND ONE OF THE FIRST TO POOP ON A TOURIST.

PERFECT FOR INSULTING

- WHISPER TALKERS ☐
- CHRONIC BANANA EATERS ☐
- BIG BIRD ☐

NATIVE AREAS

THEY ARE COMMONLY FOUND THROUGHOUT MOST OF NORTH AMERICA, JUST LIKE BEIGE 2007 TOYOTA CAMRYS.

GEOTHLYPIS TRICHAS—THAT'S EITHER THE LATIN BINOMIAL NAME OR A STEP OF EVOLUTION YOU MISSED.

LAVA HERON

TYPICALLY 18 TO 20" LONG, THESE CREEPY THINGS ARE NOTABLE FOR THEIR DARK GRAY PLUMAGE, GLOWING ORANGE EYES, AND POSTURE THAT'S REMINISCENT OF DANNY DEVITO IN 'BATMAN RETURNS' (SEE FIGURE 61).

SIGNATURE BIRD SONG

A RASPY 'SKUK-SKUK-SKUK' CALL THAT SOUNDS LIKE THE DOLPHIN FROM 'FLIPPER' TRYING TO WARN YOU OF DANGER.

PERFECT FOR INSULTING

- [ ] CHRONIC JACUZZI USERS
- [ ] ANNOYINGLY HOT FRIENDS
- [ ] A TOTINO'S PIZZA ROLL

FUN FACT: THEIR LEGS TURN BRIGHT ORANGE WHEN THEY'RE READY TO MATE—WHICH HAS TO BE AWKWARD AT WORK.

NATIVE AREAS

EXCLUSIVELY FOUND ON THE GALÁPAGOS ISLANDS—WHICH, AS IT TURNS OUT, IS DIFFERENT THAN GILLIGAN'S ISLAND.

BUTORIDES SUNDEVALLI—THAT'S EITHER THE LATIN BINOMIAL NAME OR A VICTORIAN MAGICIAN.

GIVE ME SOME SPACE, YOU LAVA HERON.
FIG. 61

WERE THOSE
EVEN WORDS,
YOU COMMON
BABBLER?
FIG. 62

COMMON BABBLER

ALTHOUGH TECHNICALLY MEASURING ABOUT 8" IN LENGTH, MOST OF THAT IS THEIR LONG, SLENDER TAIL—WHICH IS A PERFECT DISTRACTION FROM THE FACT THAT THEY ALWAYS LOOK A LITTLE WET FOR SOME REASON (SEE FIGURE 62).

SIGNATURE BIRD SONG

A LOUD, TRILLING 'TWEE-TWEE-TA-WHIT-CHU' THAT SOUNDS IDENTICAL TO THOSE EXAGGERATED CARTOON SNORES.

FUN FACT: THEY HAVE ADAPTED TO LIFE IN CITIES—IN OTHER WORDS, THEY'VE JUST LEARNED NOT TO MAKE EYE CONTACT WITH ANYONE.

PERFECT FOR INSULTING

- TIME-SHARE SALESPEOPLE ☐
- DUMB BABIES ☐
- THAT INCESSANT BROOK ☐

NATIVE AREAS

COMMON BABBLERS CAN BE FOUND THROUGHOUT INDIA. OTHER BABBLERS? THEY'RE USUALLY NEXT TO US IN COFFEE SHOPS.

ARGYA CAUDATA—THAT'S EITHER THE LATIN BINOMIAL NAME OR A PIRATE TRYING TO INSULT SOMEONE.

BUFF-THROATED WOODCREEPER

APPROXIMATELY 10 TO 11" LONG, THESE FOREST BIRDS ARE MORE DISTINCTIVE FOR THEIR REDDISH-BROWN PLUMAGE THAN THEY ARE FOR THEIR THROATS. HONESTLY, IT DOESN'T EVEN LOOK LIKE THEY WORK OUT THAT MUCH (SEE FIGURE 63).

SIGNATURE BIRD SONG

THOSE RAPID, HIGH-PITCHED 'ERRT-ERRT-ERRT' CHIRPS THAT YOUR WASHING MACHINE MAKES BEFORE THE BELT BREAKS.

PERFECT FOR INSULTING

- ☐ PEEPING TOMS
- ☐ FALL FOLIAGE AFICIONADOS
- ☐ HE-MAN

FUN FACT: THEY PEEL THE BARK OFF TREES TO FIND FOOD. MEANWHILE, WE JUST OPENED OUR 10TH KIT-KAT. SO I GUESS WE'RE BOTH TALENTED.

NATIVE AREAS

PRIMARILY FOUND IN THE HUMID EVERGREEN FORESTS OF NORTHERN SOUTH AMERICA—WHICH ARE NOT TO BE CONFUSED WITH THE HUMID EVERGREEN FORESTS OF SOUTHERN NORTH AMERICA. THOSE ARE MOSTLY JUST FULL OF METH.

FIG. 63
WHAT ARE YOU STARING AT, YOU BUFF-THROATED WOODCREEPER?

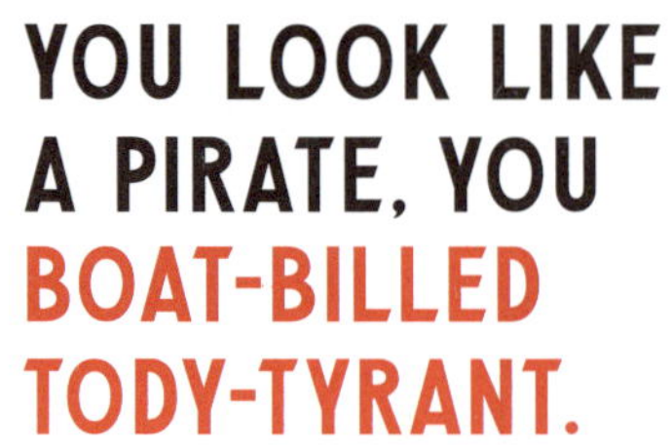

FIG. 64

BOAT-BILLED TODY-TYRANT

AT JUST 4" LONG, THESE ADORABLE LITTLE BIRDS FEATURE OLIVE-ISH WINGS AND PALE BODIES—YET NO ONE CAN STOP TALKING ABOUT THEIR WIDE, AWKWARDLY SHAPED BEAKS. TALK ABOUT UNREALISTIC BEAUTY STANDARDS (SEE FIGURE 64).

SIGNATURE BIRD SONG

A HOLLOW, YET SPORADIC 'PING' NOTE—LIKE THE SOUND OF A HIGHLY CONCERNING HEART MONITOR.

FUN FACT: THEY ARE FOND OF EATING INSECTS—ALMOST AS MUCH AS THEY ARE FOND OF OVERLY HYPHENATED NAMES.

PERFECT FOR INSULTING

- AMPHIBIAN BREEDERS ☐
- LUXURY YACHT LEASERS ☐
- MR. TOAD'S BOSS ☐

NATIVE AREAS

FOUND IN NORTHEASTERN BRAZIL, THE GUIANAS, AND, THANKS TO PUBLIC SCHOOL, A BUNCH OF OTHER MYSTERIOUS PLACES.

HEMITRICCUS JOSEPHINAE—THAT'S EITHER THE LATIN BINOMIAL NAME OR A ROMANCE NOVELIST'S PEN NAME.

RED-NECKED GREBE

USUALLY 17 TO 21" LONG, THESE BIRDS DEVELOP BRICK-RED NECKS DURING BREEDING SEASON. YET AFTERWARDS, THEY FADE TO A DULL BROWN—WHICH IS HOW WE FEEL WHEN YOU AREN'T AROUND. HA HA. THAT RHYMED (SEE FIGURE 65).

SIGNATURE BIRD SONG

BOTH MALES AND FEMALES GIVE A RAPID, WHINNYING TRILL. FEMALES, WHILE LAYING EGGS, MALES, AFTER STUBBING A TOE.

PERFECT FOR INSULTING

- [ ] TURTLENECK WEARERS
- [ ] PEOPLE WHO SAY 'WARSH'
- [ ] THE RED M&M

FUN FACT: THEY INGEST LARGE AMOUNTS OF THEIR OWN FEATHERS—AND EVEN FEED SOME OF THEM TO THEIR BABIES. THEY AREN'T SELFISH.

NATIVE AREAS

MOSTLY FOUND IN NORTHERN CLIMATES, BUT SOME HAVE MADE IT AS FAR AS BERMUDA. WE THINK. THAT TRIANGLE IS TRICKY.

PODICEPS GRISEGENA—THAT'S EITHER THE LATIN BINOMIAL NAME OR A CHARACTER ON THAT 1990s 'DINOSAURS' SITCOM.

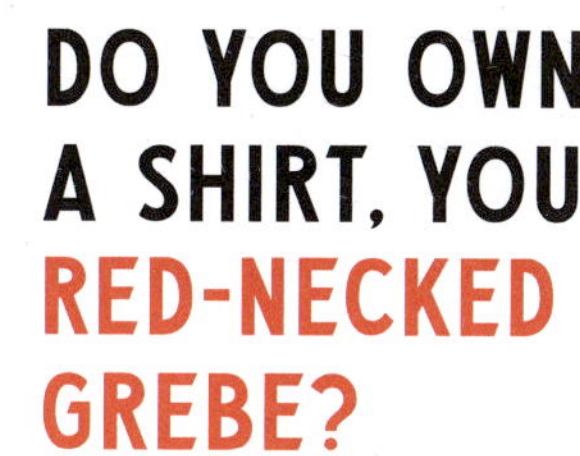

FIG. 65

FIG. 66

BUZZING FLOWERPECKER

APPROXIMATELY 3.5" LONG, WITH A GREENISH UPPER BODY, A PALE BELLY, AND A STUBBY, CURVED BILL. JOKE'S ON US THOUGH, THEY'RE GOING TO MAKE A KILLING DOING THOSE PEYRONIE'S DISEASE ADS (SEE FIGURE 66).

SIGNATURE BIRD SONG

A VIBRATING 'BZEEEPPP' SOUND—LIKE THE PANERA PAGER TELLING YOU YOUR BROCCOLI CHEDDAR BREAD BOWL IS READY.

FUN FACT: THEY ARE COMMONLY DESCRIBED AS 'DRAB-LOOKING' BY A BUNCH OF ORNITHOLOGISTS THAT RESEMBLE OLD SHOES.

PERFECT FOR INSULTING

- HELICOPTER PARENTS ☐
- INCESSANT TELEMARKETERS ☐
- RUDE FLORISTS ☐

NATIVE AREAS

PRIMARILY FOUND IN THE PHILIPPINES, WHERE THEIR SINGING IS OVERSHADOWED BY 5-YEAR-OLD KARAOKE PRODIGIES.

DICAEUM HYPOLEUCUM—THAT'S EITHER THE LATIN BINOMIAL NAME OR THE MEDICAL TERM FOR AN EXTRA POOP HOLE.

PLAIN HONEYEATER

TYPICALLY 7" LONG, THESE BIRDS ARE DISTINCTIVE FOR THE LONG, BEAUTIFUL STRIATIONS IN THEIR TAIL FEATHERS. WE'RE KIDDING. THESE SUCKERS ARE BROWN, AND NOT A MEMORABLE BROWN EITHER. PICTURE 'MEH' WITH WINGS (SEE FIGURE 67).

SIGNATURE BIRD SONG

USUALLY QUIET, WITH AN OCCASIONAL 'EE-TRT' THAT REALLY JUST SOUNDS LIKE A PARROT TRYING TO IMITATE A DONKEY.

PERFECT FOR INSULTING

- ☐ RELENTLESS OPTIMISTS
- ☐ HOLISTIC MOMS
- ☐ HUNDRED ACRE WOOD BEARS

FUN FACT: THEY HAVE BRUSH-TIPPED TONGUES THAT CAN RETRIEVE HARD-TO-REACH NECTAR—AND CAN REALLY CLEAN OUT THOSE GO-GURT TUBES.

NATIVE AREAS

FOUND IN THE MOIST TROPICAL AND SUBTROPICAL FORESTS OF NEW GUINEA. SADLY NOT FOUND? A DECENT PIÑA COLADA.

PYCNOPYGIUS IXOIDES—THAT'S EITHER THE LATIN BINOMIAL NAME OR THE ACTIVE INGREDIENT IN ANTIFUNGAL CREAMS.

FIG. 67
UGH, GROW A PERSONALITY, YOU PLAIN HONEYEATER.

FIG. 68

CHATTERING GNATWREN

ROUGHLY 4.5" LONG, THESE BROWNISH-GREEN BIRDS HAVE PALE THROATS, SLENDER BEAKS, AND TINY BALL-LIKE BODIES. THEY'RE ALSO HIGHLY ACTIVE—AND JUST LIKE YOUR CROSSFIT FRIEND, THEY DON'T SHUT UP ABOUT IT (SEE FIGURE 68).

SIGNATURE BIRD SONG

IMAGINE SOMEONE SAYING 'AHHHH' IN A VIBRATING MASSAGE CHAIR, WHILE GETTING INTERRUPTED BY LAWN SPRINKLERS.

FUN FACT: THEY COMMUNICATE WITH NEARBY BIRDS BY FLICKING THEIR LONG TAILS FROM SIDE TO SIDE. THE MESSAGE? LIKELY BUTT RELATED.

PERFECT FOR INSULTING

- KIDS THAT REFUSE COATS ☐
- BAD AUCTIONEERS ☐
- THE 'MICRO MACHINES' GUY ☐

NATIVE AREAS

USUALLY FOUND IN THE AMAZONIAN LOWLANDS OF BOLIVIA, BRAZIL, AND PERU. UNLESS THEY'RE VISITING THE IN-LAWS.

RAMPHOCAENUS STICTURUS—THAT'S EITHER THE LATIN BINOMIAL NAME OR WHAT SHAKESPEARE CALLED HIS WIENER.

FRECKLED NIGHTJAR

AROUND 11" LONG, THESE BROWN AND WHITE SPECKLED BIRDS ARE REALLY TALENTED WHEN IT COMES TO LOOKING JUST LIKE A ROCK—WHICH IS QUITE THE BACKHANDED COMPLIMENT IF YOU ASK US (SEE FIGURE 69).

SIGNATURE BIRD SONG

A SLOWLY REPEATING 'OW-WOW' SOUND—LIKE SOME REALLY LAID-BACK SECURITY ALARM GOING OFF.

PERFECT FOR INSULTING

- [ ] IRISH VAMPIRES
- [ ] SPLATTER PAINT ARTISTS
- [ ] CONAN O'BRIEN

FUN FACT: THEY TOLERATE SURFACE TEMPERATURES OF UP TO 140°F—AND, ACCORDING TO STUDIES, THAT'S ALMOST AS HOT AS YOUR MOM.

NATIVE AREAS

THEY ARE FOUND ACROSS MUCH OF SUB-SAHARAN AFRICA. YOU KNOW, WHERE THE LION SLEEPS, WELL, EVERY NIGHT.

CAPRIMULGUS TRISTIGMA—THAT'S EITHER THE LATIN BINOMIAL NAME OR A JUICE BOX-RELATED INFECTION.

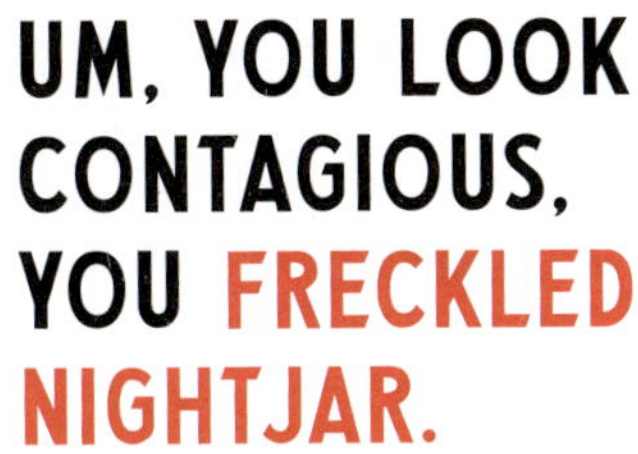

FIG. 69

FIG. 70
THAT WAS SAD, YOU DOUBLE-TOOTHED KITE.

DOUBLE-TOOTHED KITE

TYPICALLY 4" LONG, THESE TINY, DARK GRAY HAWK THINGS HAVE RUST-COLORED BELLIES AND A NOTCHED UPPER BILL. SCIENTIFICALLY SPEAKING, THEY'RE THE SNAGGLETOOTHED NANNY MCPHEE OF THE BIRD WORLD (SEE FIGURE 70).

SIGNATURE BIRD SONG

A HIGH-PITCHED WHISTLY NOISE, LIKE SOMEONE TRYING TO SAY ANY WORD STARTING IN 'S' AFTER LOSING A FRONT TOOTH.

FUN FACT: THEY FOLLOW MONKEYS AROUND, IN THE HOPE OF EATING THEIR LEFTOVERS—MUCH LIKE US WHEN KIDS HAVE CHICKEN NUGGETS.

PERFECT FOR INSULTING

- AIR-HEADED COWORKERS ☐
- TEETHING BABIES ☐
- CERTAINLY NOT MIKE TYSON ☐

NATIVE AREAS

FOUND IN THE NEOTROPICAL REALM—WHICH IS BASICALLY JUST WHERE ALL THE GOOD SEASONS OF 'SURVIVOR' WERE FILMED.

HARPAGUS BIDENTATUS—THAT'S EITHER THE LATIN BINOMIAL NAME OR THE TITLE OF A MEDIEVAL JOE BIDEN FANFIC.

SHORT-BILLED DOWITCHER

USUALLY 9 TO 12" LONG, THESE MOTTLED BROWN BIRDS MAY BE KNOWN AS SHORT—BUT THEY'RE LONG WHERE IT MATTERS. IN THEIR BEAKS AND LEGS. YOU KNOW, SO THEY CAN EAT AND SURVIVE. DON'T BE SO GROSS (SEE FIGURE 71).

SIGNATURE BIRD SONG

THAT QUICK, SQUEAKY NOISE WHEN YOU TRY TO CLEAN A SPOT OFF OF MIRROR THAT'S LOADED UP WITH WINDEX.

PERFECT FOR INSULTING

- ☐ PAYDAY LOAN LENDERS
- ☐ NEW AGE SPIRITUALISTS
- ☐ HOWARD THE DUCK

FUN FACT: THEIR BILL IS ONLY 'SHORT' WHEN IT'S COMPARED TO THE LONG-BILLED DOWITCHER. LIKE A 'SHORT-CASHED MILLIONAIRE.'

NATIVE AREAS

SPREAD WIDELY AROUND THE WETLANDS OF NORTH AMERICA, THEY LIKELY LIVE WITH A PERPETUAL CASE OF RAISIN-TOES.

PREFER TO USE THE LATIN BINOMIAL NAME? MAYBE WASH YOUR HAIR FIRST, YOU LIMNODROMUS GRISEUS.

KEEP DREAMING, YOU SHORT-BILLED DOWITCHER.
FIG. 71

STAY AWAY FROM MY LEFTOVERS, YOU SPOTTED TOWHEE.
FIG. 72

SPOTTED TOWHEE

ROUGHLY 5" LONG, WITH JET BLACK UPPER BODIES AND STARK WHITE BELLIES. YET THESE BIRDS ARE MOST DISTINCTIVE FOR THE BRIGHT ORANGE PATCHES UNDER THEIR WINGS THAT LOOK LIKE HAIR PLUGS FROM ED SHEERAN (SEE FIGURE 72).

SIGNATURE BIRD SONG

DISTINCTIVE FOR THEIR PROLONGED, MRS. DOUBTFIRE-ESQE SINGSONGS THAT SOUND JUST LIKE 'DRINK-YOUR-TEA.'

FUN FACT: FEMALES WILL RAISE UP TO THREE BROODS EACH YEAR—DON'T WORRY, THEIR REALITY SHOW HAS ALREADY BEEN GREENLIT BY TLC.

PERFECT FOR INSULTING

- TOW TRUCK DRIVERS ☐
- PEOPLE WITH CHICKEN POX ☐
- VARIOUS DALMATIANS ☐

NATIVE AREAS

MOSTLY FOUND IN THE WESTERN PARTS OF NORTH AMERICA. THEY REFUSE TO GET TOO FAR FROM A WHATABURGER.

PIPILO MACULATUS—THAT'S EITHER THE LATIN BINOMIAL NAME OR THE PATRON SAINT OF WIND INSTRUMENTS.

FRECKLE-BREASTED THORNBIRD

APPROXIMATELY 8.5" LONG, THESE BROWNISH, SPECKLED BIRDS ARE EXCELLENT NEST BUILDERS—AND A CAUTIONARY VISION FROM THE FUTURE UNLESS YOU STOP TANNING LIKE IT'S AN OLYMPIC SPORT (SEE FIGURE 73).

SIGNATURE BIRD SONG

SLOWLY DESCENDING 'PSEP-PSEP-KLEEK-KLEEK' SQUEAKS—LIKE A TALKATIVE MOUSE FALLING DOWN A WELL.

PERFECT FOR INSULTING

- ☐ NURSES GIVING SHOTS
- ☐ DRY ROTISSERIE CHICKENS
- ☐ THE WENDY'S MASCOT

FUN FACT: THEY CONSTRUCT ELABORATE NESTS OUT OF SHARP THORNS AND TWIGS TO KEEP OUT PREDATORS—AND SOLICITORS.

NATIVE AREAS

FOUND ACROSS CENTRAL SOUTH AMERICA—PRIMARILY IN PARTS OF ARGENTINA, BOLIVIA, AND PARAGUAY. THEY'RE KNOWN TO INHABIT EVERYTHING FROM DRY SAVANNAS TO FORESTED MARSHES. BUT THEY AREN'T PSYCHOPATHS—EVEN THEY WON'T RENT BOTTOM FLOOR APARTMENTS.

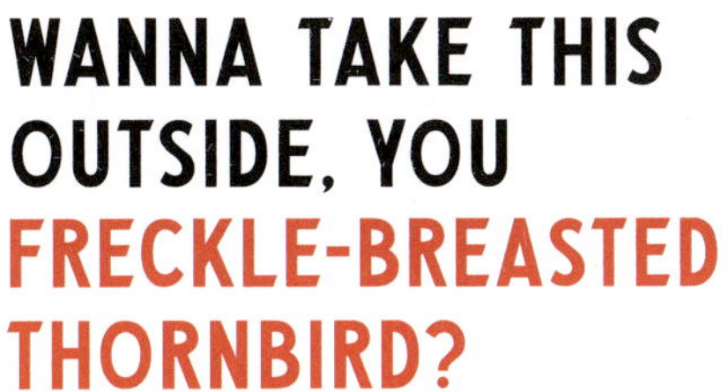

FIG. 73

FIG. 74

AMERICAN COOT

ABOUT 15 TO 17" LONG, THESE DARK-GRAY BIRDS ARE OFTEN MISTAKEN FOR DUCKS. WHICH IS INSULTING. SEE, THEY HAVE LOBED TOES, NOT WEBBED FEET—SO THEY CAN WALK BETTER ON DRY LAND THAN THOSE DUCK IDIOTS (SEE FIGURE 74).

SIGNATURE BIRD SONG

IF YOU HEAR SOMEBODY CALLING YOU 'PRIK' FROM THE BUSHES, THERE'S A 50 PERCENT CHANCE IT'S JUST THIS BIRD.

FUN FACT: IT'S JUST A MYTH THAT COOTS DON'T TASTE GOOD—BUT IT REALLY HELPS WITH THAT WHOLE 'NOT GETTING SHOT' THING.

PERFECT FOR INSULTING

- BALD EAGLES ☐
- ROADSIDE FIREWORK STANDS ☐
- THAT ONE RACIST UNCLE ☐

NATIVE AREAS

FOUND IN THE WARM FRESHWATER WETLANDS OF NORTH AMERICA—JUST LIKE THOSE BRAIN-EATING AMOEBAS. USA! USA!

FULICA AMERICANA—THAT'S EITHER THE LATIN BINOMIAL NAME OR WHAT THEY CALL AMERICAN GIRL DOLLS IN ITALY.

LOWLAND SOOTY BOUBOU

USUALLY 7 TO 8.5" LONG, THESE BLUISH-BLACK BIRDS ARE REMARKABLY DARK. THEY'RE KNOWN TO FREQUENT FORESTS, BUT THEY, AND THEIR BIG SOULLESS EYES, ARE PROBABLY BETTER SUITED FOR YOUR NIGHTMARES (SEE FIGURE 75).

SIGNATURE BIRD SONG

SOUNDS LIKE SOMEONE RUBBING THE RIM OF A WINE GLASS WITH THEIR FINGER—BUT LIKE, IN A TREE OR SOMETHING.

PERFECT FOR INSULTING

- ☐ DICKENSIAN ORPHANS
- ☐ SHADY AUTO MECHANICS
- ☐ PIG-PEN

FUN FACT: THEIR BILLS START OUT WHITE AND THEN DARKEN WITH AGE—WHICH IS MUCH LIKE OUR OUTLOOK ON LIFE.

NATIVE AREAS

REGRETTABLY FOUND IN THE MOIST FORESTS, MOIST SWAMPS, AND MOIST SHRUBLANDS OF CENTRAL AFRICA. ICK.

LANIARIUS LEUCORHYNCHUS—THAT'S EITHER THE LATIN BINOMIAL NAME OR THE DR. PHIL OF GREEK PHILOSOPHERS.

WASH YOUR HANDS, YOU LOWLAND SOOTY BOUBOU.
FIG. 75

INDEX OF BIRDS / INSULTS

INDEX OF BIRDS/INSULTS

INDEX OF BIRDS / INSULTS

BRASSMONKEYGOODS.COM

×

@BRASSMONKEYGOODS